ONE
DIVINE
MOMENT

Robert E. Coleman is the Sollie E. McCreless Professor of Evangelism at Asbury Theological Seminary, and also serves as President of Christian Outreach. Other Revell books by Dr. Coleman are *The Master Plan of Evangelism* and *Dry Bones Can Live Again.*

ONE
DIVINE
MOMENT

Edited by
Robert E. Coleman

Fleming H. Revell Company
Old Tappan, New Jersey

Copyright © 1970 by Fleming H. Revell Company
All Rights Reserved
Library of Congress Catalog Card Number: 71-137444
Printed in the United States of America

*Give me one divine moment when God acts
and I say that moment is far superior to all
the human efforts of man throughout the centuries.*

DENNIS F. KINLAW
President, Asbury College

Contents

Foreword

The unusual revival which came to Asbury College early in 1970 and spread to scores of campuses across America is evidence that God is still at work in His world, lifting men and women out of self-centeredness, secularism, and boredom.

It came at a time when radical students were striving desperately to upset the educational equilibrium of our nation with burning, destroying property, rock throwing, and other forms of violence. The Bible says, ". . . where sin abounded, grace did much more abound," and His grace was displayed in a phenomenal way on many campuses, even while other campuses were on the brink of chaos.

With the Lord, it is usually in the worst of times that the best things happen. The Protestant Reformation, the Wesleyan Revival, and the Great Awakening in America in the nineteenth century are examples.

Perhaps the eruptions of revival which swept through a segment of our college youth in the early months of 1970 are harbingers of what the Holy Spirit is ready, able and willing to do, throughout the world, if Christians will dare to pay the price.

It is my prayer that what began at Asbury College, and spread like a fire to other campuses, will encourage believers everywhere to claim the promise: "If my people, which are called by my name, shall humble themselves, and pray, and seek my face, and turn from their wicked ways; then will I hear from heaven, and will forgive their sin, and will heal their land" (II Chronicles 7:14).

BILLY GRAHAM

"And it shall come to pass in the last days, saith God, I will pour out of my Spirit upon all flesh . . ." (Acts 2:17 KJV).

Preface

All moments in history are not the same. Some loom large like Mount Everest, towering high above what surrounds them. For decades and centuries afterward men point back to these moments as decisive in human destiny. Usually these are times when men take some new and bold action. But there are moments when God decisively acts to reveal Himself and His purposes. In such a time the moment not only teems with present significance, but it can fill the future with new meaning and radiance.

One of these divine moments came on February 3, 1970. The visitation occurred in Wilmore, Kentucky, a small town near Lexington. While many students across America were burning down buildings and rioting in the streets, students in this college community were strangely drawn to their knees to pray. It was as if the campus had been suddenly invaded by another Power. Classes were forgotten. Academic work came to a standstill. In a way awesome to behold, God had taken over the campus. Caught up in the wonder of it, a thousand students remained for days in the college auditorium—not to demand more freedom or to protest

13

the Establishment, but to confess their sin and to sing the praises of their Saviour.

"This could be the start of something big," one veteran newscaster covering the phenomenon told his television audience. Then he asked his viewers to put down their newspapers, stop whatever they were doing and watch the revival scene which he had filmed earlier in the day. He concluded, "I've never seen anything like this. I still can't believe it."

Indeed, it may be difficult to believe. In this age of unbelief, Divine intervention in the affairs of our rebellious world does seem unlikely. But the reality of it has been confirmed by thousands of people whose lives felt the breath of God. Fires of faith were lighted that have since spread around the world. And still are burning at this hour.

This divine moment did not come about through human scheduling or preaching. Instead, it came as people opened themselves to the living God, and received the forgiveness and cleansing which God alone can give. The change wrought in them was and is too great to keep secret. It must be shared. Thus one man's divine moment becomes the gateway through which others may come to know the same experience.

Attention from the beginning of this movement has centered upon the quiet working of the Holy Spirit. To emphasize His dominance, wherever possible we have not used names of the human personalities involved. However, the role of unnamed individuals and their testimonies have been reported accurately. For those who may be interested in further information, a selected bibliography of published news items and feature stories about the revival may be found at the back of the book.

Grateful acknowledgment is due to the many persons who have compiled the story. Their number adds perspective and variety to the account. Each in his own way gives authentic insight to a moment which uniquely belongs to God. The narrative throbs with wonder and excitement. It is fresh. It is for real. As few stories of our generation, it breathes the life of true revival. Reading these pages can be a joyful experience that will thrill the heart with hope.

All royalties from the sale of the book will be given to a scholarship fund for students at Asbury College and Asbury Theological Seminary.

ROBERT E. COLEMAN

"When the day of Pentecost had come, they were all together in one place. And suddenly a sound came from heaven like the rush of a mighty wind, and it filled all the house where they were sitting" (Acts 2:1, 2 RSV).

1

God in Our Midst

HOWARD A. HANKE

Tuesday, the third of February, dawned like any other winter day in Wilmore, Kentucky. A cold wind whipped through the tall, barren trees on the campus of Asbury College. No one could have guessed that soon the little school would be caught up in a demonstration of divine love that would have repercussions to the ends of the earth.

Casual chatter occupied the conversation of students as they hurried to the 10 A.M. chapel service. Walking up the steps of the stately Hughes Auditorium one could see chiseled on the cornerstone: FOLLOW PEACE WITH ALL MEN AND HOLINESS WITHOUT WHICH NO MAN SHALL SEE THE LORD. This Scripture verse expressed the aspirations of the college, and gave insight to her heritage. But the admonition was scarcely in the thinking of the nearly 1,000 students as they rushed to get in their assigned seats before the bell.

The program that morning did not follow its customary worship pattern. The dean of the college, who was the scheduled speaker, did not feel impressed to preach. Instead, he felt led to have students participate in a testimony meeting. This practice is not strange to Asbury College where students are encouraged to give voice to their inner faith.

For some time a small group of students had been involved in a vigorous devotional discipline. It included getting up a half hour earlier than usual each morning for prayer, Bible study and to plan specific ministries during the day. Many of these persons had entered into more meaningful experiences with God, and their witness was having an effect upon others in the college. In addition, various groups—large and small—had been meeting at different times to pray for spiritual awakening. All of this had contributed to an air of expectancy on the campus. A few students were even stating prophetically that a great outpouring of the Holy Spirit was imminent.

The dean opened the testimony service by sharing his own experience with God. He then invited others to do the same. Quickly a number of students arose in various areas of the sanctuary. Their testimonies were fervent and reflected deep heart-searching. Clichés were totally absent. Each person seemed intent upon sharing an up-to-date report on what God was doing in his or her life.

One recalcitrant senior shocked the audience by confessing, "I'm not believing that I'm standing here telling you what God has done for me. I've wasted my time in college up to now, but Christ has met me and I'm different. Last night the Holy Spirit flooded in and filled my life. Now, for the first time ever, I am excited about being a Christian! I wouldn't want to go back to the emptiness of yesterday for anything." Others followed. Everyone sensed that something unusual was happening. God seemed very near.

Sensing the mandate of the moment, near the close of the allotted chapel hour one of the professors slipped to the platform and expressed his feeling that any students who wanted to pray should feel free to come to the altar. There was no pleading or cajoling—just the quiet reminder that the altar was open.

(Perhaps it should be explained that traditionally the altar is where man meets and communes with God. In the college auditorium, as in many churches, it is represented by a long kneeling bench located between the front pews and the platform. The furnishing is a carry-over from the Old Testament altar on which a penitent presented his sacrifice to symbolize a complete dedication of his life to Jehovah. The Christian sees in it now the cross where Christ offered Himself as the perfect sacrifice for our sins. It is only natural, then, for the kneeling rail to become a sacred place of prayer.)

No sooner had the invitation been extended than a mass of students moved forward. The congregation began singing "Just As I Am." There was not room for all who wanted to pray at the altar. Many had to kneel in the front seats of the auditorium. Their prayers were mingled with heartfelt contrition and outbursts of joy. It was evident that God was moving upon His people in power. The presence of the Lord was so real that all other interests seemed unimportant. The bell sounded for classes to begin, but went unheeded.

At the time of this first invitation to pray there were still a number of students standing, ready to testify. As scores of students flocked forward to pray, these young people made their way to the edge of the platform, hoping yet to be able to give their testimony. After a short wait one girl strode toward the podium and asked the professor in charge if she could please say something. He stepped aside. As she finished, a second student stepped forward.

Those who had come to the altar—after a time of prayer—rose, joining those on the platform and with tears made confessions. These acknowledgments ranged from cheating and theft to having animosity, prejudice and jealousy. Some made their way to individuals in the congregation to ask forgiveness and to make restitution. Old enmities were melted with the fervent love of God. Frequently these encounters of reconciliation resulted in experiences of joy and gladness. Some shook hands while others embraced. Often having obtained a new relationship with God, students would raise their fingers in the peace symbol, a V for victory sign.

A long line of students began to form as each waited his turn to tell what God had done in his heart. Students in all classes from freshmen to seniors poured out their souls, asking forgiveness and exhorting others to heed the call of God. As the confessions were made, other students streamed to the front, filling the altar and front seats.

This intense divine manifestation continued into the noon hour. One faculty member reported that he went to the dining hall for a scheduled divisional meeting. When he found only a few diners in the place ordinarily filled, he came back to the chapel, where people were more concerned with the divine bread of heaven than food for the body.

Occasionally students and faculty with special vocal talents were led by the Spirit to come to the microphone to sing their testimony. Other times someone in the congregation might lift a familiar hymn which would soon be caught up by all. When the tide was running high, the singing congregation often would witness to their faith by raising their arms heavenward. One of the most beautiful of the musical moments was when members of the Women's Glee Club stood in their places around the auditorium and sang with fervor "When I Survey the Wondrous Cross."

The service continued on into the afternoon as announcement was made that classes were suspended for the rest of the day. A sweet gentle current of the Holy Spirit circulated within the congregation giving a feeling of warmth around the heart. Students continued to testify and pray with no abatement of earnestness. Toward the supper hour some began to leave, but the building began to fill again as the marathon service entered into the evening. At times nearly every seat in the 1,550 capacity auditorium was occupied. Some people were standing around the walls. Others were looking on from the doorways, sometimes virtually blocking the exits.

In the sanctuary there was continual movement to and from the altar. At times the whole front of the auditorium was crowded with people on their knees; some praying, some giving counsel, some just rejoicing in the Lord. All the while on the platform there was the unceasing stream of people publicly declaring the wonderful works of God.

The classrooms in the basement served as meeting places for special prayer groups or afforded a quiet Bethel for someone to meditate upon heavenly things. It was common to see students seated or kneeling together—two by two with an open Bible—praying or discussing the things of God. Not infrequently all the rooms were filled and persons were to be seen praying in the lower assembly hall. They knelt on the floor by chairs and benches as if they were there alone. No one seemed to be bothered when people passed by. The spirit of unity was so real that everyone felt a common interest in and sympathy for the spiritual needs of others.

During the first day some of the 450 seminary students were deeply moved by the divine visitation of Asbury College and began to yearn for the same spiritual renewal on their campus across the street. An all-night prayer meeting was quickly called. This vigil intensified the burden for revival that some had felt for many months.

The next morning at the regular seminary chapel service it happened. As at the college, this program, too, was unusual in that no formal preaching was planned. Rather, the time was scheduled as a hymn-sing. When one student stood up to relate how the revival had affected his life, many under the power of the Spirit began to move to the altar. There followed the now familiar pattern of hearts melting in the refining fire of God's presence.

Some of the students and faculty came to the pulpit and openly acknowledged faults and spiritual needs. Resentments, hidden jealousies, lustful desires, worldly attitudes of all kinds were brought out into the open. A sin often confessed related to the indifferent way the holy things of God had been treated. As one graduate student expressed it, "I've become nonchalant about this whole business of being a Christian and of witnessing to others." Asking for the prayers of his associates, he fell at the altar to seek forgiveness and to make a new and deeper surrender of his life.

The service continued on into the afternoon. Some classes tried to meet, but many students remained in the chapel where the divine presence was still so much in evidence. By the next day all classes were officially cancelled for the rest of the week.

The tone of the seminary revival was generally more subdued than at the college, but no less genuine. Testimonies of the students were touched with a tenderness and a love which could only come from men and women who had been with Christ.

Most of the men in the seminary are married, and it was inspiring to note how many of them brought their wives into the services. It was a common sight to see couples holding hands and walking down the aisle to kneel at the altar together. After renewing their love for God, they would rise with tear-dimmed eyes and embrace, evidencing a renewal of their love for each other.

Over the weekend, the seminary phase of the revival merged with the college where the main activities continued around the clock without any letup. High peaks in attendance would come in the evening hours when the main sanctuary was crowded. Even at 2:30 A.M. there might still be 300 people in the chapel at prayer. Their numbers would dwindle to less than a hundred before sunrise. Then after breakfast the building would begin to fill again.

Day after day the campus community was absorbed in only one thing: getting right with God and seeking His will. Divine prerogatives transcended all other considerations. Being present at the services seemed to be the most important thing at the moment. Radio, TV, parties, ball games, and other activities did not hold any appeal. One person was heard to say, "I have gone on a complete radio and TV fast." Time did not seem to matter. Many students were so engrossed in the Spirit that they stayed in the chapel a better part of the whole week.

During the services people were free to do their own thing as the Spirit led. A few faculty members were always on hand to help direct witnesses to the microphone and to make announcements. But they did not try to manipulate the services according to any prescribed schedule. The amazing thing is that in the face of such liberty there was no disorder. A few times something may have been said in a testimony that was out of place, but invariably when this happened, the Holy Spirit quickly got the situation under control.

Occasionally the pattern of witnessing was interrupted by special seasons of prayer in response to the many requests coming in. Telegrams, letters and phone calls contained urgent appeals for prayer from all over the United States and Canada. Reports of the revival outreach in other communities also were shared from time to time. When the news of some new victory was heard, people would break forth in shouts of praise while the congregation would pick up the strains of the organ and with uplifted hands, would join in singing "To God be the Glory."

Hundreds of visitors were attracted to the campus through news reports of the revival. Some came from as far away as California, Florida and Canada. Many of these strangers were greatly stirred by the Holy Spirit and came to the platform to testify of their own renewal. One person said he heard about the revival over his car radio, and his curiosity led him to drive by the campus. He was so stricken by the power of God that he himself found a wonderful Christian experience at the altar. A couple intended to stop for a short visit and stayed a week. Another car full of people were on their way to spend a vacation in West Virginia with relatives, but they were so overcome with the revival spirit that they spent all their vacation at Asbury.

Many townspeople joined in the revival, especially the teenagers. Some youth who previously had little interest in religion were converted and began to talk to their friends about Christ. One of these witnessing youth was awakened from a deep sleep at 3 A.M. one morning. Towering over him was a bearded, shaggy-haired hippy friend who said, "I'm ready to go to the altar." The two boys went to Hughes Auditorium to pray, and before long the friend was testifying to the saving grace of Jesus.

On Sunday, several of the local churches dismissed their regular services to encourage everyone to go to the revival. There was standing room only as more than 1,600 persons jammed the building. One of the most moving hours of the week came that morning when one of the local pastors took his place at the pulpit and poured out his agonized soul and confessed his shortcomings. He was followed by his wife, who confessed at length her unhappy state of mind about being a pastor's wife in Wilmore. Both testified to a renewal of grace and infilling of divine love. The pastor called several people by name and made his peace with them. Following this demonstration, the president of Asbury College suggested that there should be more than one hundred adults among the faculty, staff and town community who should come to the altar and make things right with God and man. Immediately a mass of people moved forward, filling the front section of the auditorium and front aisles. Many prayed and wept with deep emotion and afterward came to the platform to make apology to those whom they had wronged and against whom they had resentment. The spiritual and social healing which occurred on that Sunday morning has solved more problems than any other event in the town for many years.

The spontaneous revival continued into the chapel period on Tuesday, February 10. Many were still in line to give their witness. Some had appeared before the congregation several times, giving progress reports on their own spiritual development or reporting on how God had worked through their witness.

The administration decided to resume classes at the end of the period. However, the auditorium was kept open for prayer and agreement was made to have a nightly meeting. Students continued to come and go through the day and into the night. Shortly before 3 A.M. on Wednesday morning the last student left the sanctuary. For 185 hours—without any interruption—the services had continued! During all this time there was no pressure, no scheduled meetings, no paid advertising, no offering, no invocation, no prelude or postlude, and no benediction.

And no one tried to compile any statistics. It was felt that this would be out of keeping with the spirit of the revival. But most of the students on the campus of the college and seminary knelt at the altar, and there were thousands of other persons who made a similar dedication. The whole spiritual tone of the campus was completely changed.

The lights in Hughes Auditorium still have not been turned out. Even now, months later, a few people gather each evening to pray, witness, and rejoice together. Often these meetings last into the midnight hours, with visitors not infrequently being helped on to God. Also during most hours of the day someone may still be seen entering the chapel. They kneel to pray for a few minutes, then leave. Others just sit and stare at the altar so rife with precious memories. If one looks closely, tears may be seen coursing down their cheeks.

Perhaps those tears express more eloquently than words what has happened. There is no human vocabulary that can capture the full dimension of one divine moment. In some ways, it seems almost like a dream—yet it happened. We saw it with our eyes. In a way impossible to describe, God was in our midst. Those of us who were there can never look upon the things of this world quite the same.

". . . the morning stars sang together, and all the sons of God shouted for joy" (Job 38:7 RSV).

2

A Student's Diary of Revival

JEFF BLAKE

(God came during those days. The God of the Universe made His way to a remote spot on earth and I, one of His three billion children on this planet, found myself in the midst of one of His great divine moments in this century.

My natural desire was to be a part of this transaction. My second desire was to capture the moment with written words of description and reflection. Out of a burning heart came the words that follow.

"For we cannot but speak the things which we have seen and heard" [Acts 4:20 KJV].)

February 3, 1970   I sit in the middle of a contemporary Pentecost. A few moments ago there came a spontaneous movement of the Holy Spirit. I have never witnessed such a mighty outpouring of God upon His people. The scene is unbelievable. The altar has been flooding with needy souls time and time again. Witness is abundant. Release—Freedom—There are tears. Repentence—Joy unspeakable—Embracing—Spontaneous applause when a soul celebrates. A thousand hearts lifted in songs of praise and adoration to a Mighty God.

Forgiveness—Expressions of hidden guilt and resentments. God is convicting His children. No sheer emotion. No psychology to get people to the altar. Singing—Shouting—The song, "How Great Thou Art."

Two close friends are making their way to the altar. Fill their cups, Lord. Give them victory.

12:30 P.M. Two and one-half hours have passed. A joyous religion. Hands in the air. Pointed toward God—He never fails. A brother and a sister at the altar. Friends, couples, roommates at the altar.

Three hours have passed. "Turn Your Eyes Upon Jesus."
My old roommate has found the Victory. He is urging other friends to rid themselves of the old trash and garbage that claim their lives. He says, "Shovel out the trash."

Basketball players with their coach at the altar.

A girl is singing "Broken Pieces." Too, a song with these words, "He is my reason for living."
Black people, white people, God's people.
Prayer request for a mother who left God two years ago.
The Peace sign expressed. A Spanish girl singing, "He Touched Me." Surely, the Heavenly Father has touched His children in a rare and marvelous manner this day. Father, continue to touch me and show me your Way.
Hands in the air. A boy from California who says, "Praise God, I've kicked the habit." Applause. Somehow I believe that God approves of this form of expressed joy.

28

A boy from Africa is speaking. His accent is difficult to discern. He is saying, "A day—what a day this has been!" He concluded his words with an arm outstretched and the words, "Brother, Hail." We are brothers. Called to live in one family under God.

Five hours have passed. 2:55 P.M. Again, the song, "How Great Thou Art."

We're singing "My Saviour's Love." "Pass Me Not" with the words, "Whom have I on earth beside Thee, Whom in Heaven but Thee?"

Souls still seeking at the altar.

A girl is witnessing to the truth that God has touched her eyes and now she sees people as they really are. The story in the Gospel according to Mark comes to mind. We sometimes need the second touch of Christ if we are to truly relate to our brothers. Needs are so great. God, touch our eyes. Touch our eyes.

My roommate has not moved in five hours from his seat.

One is witnessing who has found a real purpose in life.

I have a marvelous sight in view. I have seen the hearts of Asburians opened today. Laid bare. A new sense of honesty and integrity. This truth is refreshing.

A foreign student longs to go back to her island home in the Pacific and tell her people of our Lord. To her American friends she is saying, "Your people are my people."

"Go home to your friends, and tell them how much the Lord has done for you, and how he has had mercy on you" (Mark 5:19 RSV).

A brilliant student is witnessing to the sweetness of his relationship with Christ. He is saying, "Christ is no longer an option. He is a necessity."

Six hours have passed.

A man from Detroit, Michigan, just drove into Wilmore. He has now come to the platform to sing. He speaks of wasted years. My soul grieves for those who are wastefully spending their lives without our Lord. I think of names. O God, send your Spirit into these hearts. The man is singing, we are at worship, and God must be very thrilled with the movement in this place.

What a sweet Spirit there is here, and I know it's the Lord's.

A poem from a student about the love of God. People still at the altar.

While the youth of our world demonstrate, let us demonstrate for Christ.

"Just A Closer Walk With Thee."

Seven hours have passed. Eight hours. Weeping, sobbing, intense prayer.

Seeking God. "Seek the Lord while He may be found, call upon Him while he is near" (Isaiah 55:6 RSV).

A seminary student yearns for God to move in the seminary.

There is a quiet, yet beautiful Spirit here right now. Unusual sweet Spirit.

Some man is sobbing intensely.

A boy is singing "It Took A Miracle."

The altar is filled with seekers. People are kneeling in front seats.

A friend just turned to me and said, "This is something I will always treasure." Surely we will always treasure these moments.

Nine hours have passed.

Nine seekers at the altar at this moment.

The song "Without Him." Victory for one of the seekers.

How quietly and reverently the Spirit is working.

The congregation is singing "Without Him."

A local high school student is speaking. He was praying at the altar for his mother, brother, and sister. When he arose from prayer, some of his family were at the altar.

"Wait upon the Lord." Life is not life without Him.

One girl has been at the altar for nearly an hour. She doesn't seem to be able to find release. Help her, Lord.

A graduate of Asbury College prayed, "Forgive me. Forgive me." Conversion followed.

Now twelve hours have passed since it all began.

Ten souls at the altar.

Love is immature if one loves another person just to get something in return.

"It's real, it's real. I know it's real."

Fourteen souls at the altar. God is great.

A poem: "I love Jesus and He loves me. I am proud of it and so is He."

The song "Jesus Use Me."

Intense prayers now that God would open the doors of Brazil to a couple who are called there to the mission field.

Seventeen souls at the altar. A growing congregation.

A trio is singing "When Jesus Comes." Glorious news, *HE HAS COME!*

We have simply ignored God. Herein lies one of the real trage-
dies of life. We have simply ignored Him. Set us free. O God, until
we will one Will.

These are the very precious and quiet moments of the Spirit.
Twenty-nine people at the altar.

Thirteen hours have passed. 11:10 P.M. "What A Friend We
Have In Jesus." Thirty-nine at the altar.

Prayers are being lifted for churches that are in desperate need
of revival.
A lovely saxophone is playing "Take My Hand Precious Lord."
Now the congregation joins in the singing. Weeping among sev-
eral people.
"My Jesus I Love Thee." Many memories in that song. How
God has blessed!
Fourteen hours have passed. Midnight. A new day is about to
dawn.
A report of a nurse who was saved in a Lexington hospital to-
night. There is great rejoicing in this place.
The music alone plays "Grace That Is Greater Than All Our
Sin."
At midnight—Hughes Auditorium—The Heart of God must
look on with great joy.

The Psalmist said, "I commune with my heart in the night; I
meditate and search my spirit" (Psalm 77:6 RSV).

February 4, 1970 My roommate is on the platform to witness.
His words, "I knew if I did not stand to witness it would be as if I

shook my fist in the face of God. I just want to say, 'Praise the Lord.' "

Thirty-four souls at the altar.

Three hundred–four hundred people present as this new day dawns.

Romans 8:38–39. An unusual manifestation of joy right now. Victory.

The president of the senior class has been filled with the Spirit.

12:50 A.M. I'm thinking of Paul in prison at midnight.

Fifteen or sixteen hours have passed. I've lost count.

How beautiful is the congregational singing of "Blessed Assurance." Jesus is indeed our very own this night.

One is saying, "The impossible is possible."

(With these words I left Hughes for the night and returned to the dorm. My roommate and I had a wonderful season of prayer beside our bed. I remember his words as he concluded his prayer. His words seemed descriptive of the day that had just ended. He said to God, "Thank you so very much that this day has come." The day, the long unforgettable day, had ended. A new life had begun.)

One day and two hours have passed. Slightly after noon on this Wednesday, the 4th of February. Bright skies. Bitterly cold day in the snow, however.

Three souls bowed low in prayer at the altar.

A teacher at the college is witnessing. Seven people waiting to witness.

Many souls have been here through the night.

Word comes that the revival has spread to the seminary.

A very wayward boy has just made his way to the altar. There is rejoicing. I tell you it is a real thrill to see someone make such a move for his God. How the Heavens must be rejoicing this glad day.

Fourteen at the altar. Now, eighteen.

Exactly twenty-six hours have passed. The altar has just been flooded with souls.

Thirty or forty at the altar. Hallelujah!

I remember this morning at three o'clock. My roommate and I had already gone to bed and we could hear singing in Hughes. A glorious sound. Heavenly music.

Deep repentance. 1:15 P.M. Twenty-three at the altar. A minister from Georgia is telling of his filling by the Holy Spirit.

"My heart is steadfast, O God, my heart is steadfast" (Psalm 108:1 RSV)!

Unusual spirit of holiness at this moment. Many souls at the altar. Sobbing.

A soldier who returned from Viet Nam recently is speaking. He witnesses to the cleansing of God in his sinful life.

A senior from the seminary is speaking. He found release last night in the service.

There is a sweet, sweet Spirit in this place.

Twenty-eight hours have passed.

God is so present that one cannot get around Him.

Prayers for a boy who is losing his sight.

Forty-one people at the altar. 400–500 people here in Hughes.

Witness: "Me and Jesus all the way."
There is always a bigger blessing waiting.

Galatians 5. "Amazing Grace." "When we've been there ten thousand years, we've no less days to sing God's praise than when we'd first begun."
"To God Be The Glory." Prayers for Christian schools. Prayers for a family who has lost a loved one.
5 o'clock and eighteen at the altar. 6 o'clock and twenty-one at the altar.

Prayers for a lost brother. The witness of two girls who went out into the community of Wilmore to witness and brought back news of victory.

Nearing eight o'clock on this Wednesday. "Great Is Thy Faithfulness." Over one thousand people are present. The altar is overflowing.

A layman with IBM is witnessing. He is now singing "For He is so precious to me." Over a thousand souls are here. The altars are filled. Rejoicing—Hands in the air—Thirty-five hours have passed.
How strange it seems to sit in the middle of so glorious a sight.

Human pride is a huge stumbling block.
A great crowd at the altar.

February 5, 1970 (A fresh snow fell on the earth on this particular day in Wilmore. Even as God was making all things new in His creation, He was moving actively in the lives of people in Hughes Auditorium, in dorm rooms, all over the Asbury campus.)

9:50 A.M. Forty-eight hours have passed. Almost 1,500 people here in Hughes.

The altar is filled. Several people are waiting to give their witnesses. Some are witnessing to the clear, beautiful experience of God in lives. A loving God who picks people up out of the low places in life. A marvelous sight—Supernatural—This is the way God planned it.

A description of a Christian in Japan who was "The Presence of Christ." What a lovely word to be said of one who bears the name "Christian."

There is the keeping power of the blood of Christ which saves.

Emotional excitement is not the answer. We must confess our sin.

A witness: "It works. Thank God, it works."

One is preparing to witness who has been much in need. I am told that in the early hours of this day, just before dawn, God made the great contact with him. Now, he is one with his Lord. Prayer does work. Prayer changes people.

An amazing sight: Forty-eight hours have passed and the altar is still being flooded with weary souls. Simply amazing . . .

I John 5:14, 15. I John 4:14–17. The marvelous experience of perfect love.

A word of challenge to the preachers from Dean Reynolds: "Guard your call to preach with Holy jealousy." Ephesians 3:16–21. Sixty hours have passed. Incredible.

We've just sung "All Hail The Power of Jesus Name." It seems as if we are at the feet of our Lord. There is a spirit of broken selfhood.

The Old Ship of Zion is sailing along. Heaven must be in a grand Jubilee.

We've just sung "Amazing Grace." "Ten thousand years. . . ." Such rejoicing. Such rejoicing. Brotherly love abounds.

After midnight. Running to the altar. "Blessed Assurance." Electrifying moments. A grand jubilee. We are in the presence of God. Awe—Wonder—Love—An unspeakable sense of His nearness.

February 6, 1970 Revival has its high moments. Moments of exaltation. And its quiet moments when the Holy Spirit hovers over people. On this Friday morning there is a very precious spirit here in Hughes. It is quiet. God is working very beautifully in hearts this morning. There is no fear, no anxiety. The Spirit is working very quietly.

10:05 A.M. Seventy-two hours have passed. "The morning stars sang together, and all the sons of God shouted for joy" (Job 38:7 RSV).

We are highly favored. One in these days is humbled by the opportunity to be present when God chose to work. We are unworthy of so great an outpouring of His Spirit.

7:10 P.M. Twenty-one people at the altar. Quiet—Descending Spirit of God here tonight.

Some are witnessing to the truth that they wanted much more in their Christian lives than what they were experiencing.

Revival has spread to other Christian campuses. This revival is taking a national form. O, for revival on secular campuses!

Prayers for a youth rally in Norfolk, Virginia.

The auditorium is filling fast. Many at the altar.

Romans 10:9, 10. Word comes of the urgent need of revival on other Christian college campuses. Prayers for a secular campus in Louisiana. 84 hours have passed.

"Bless the Lord, O my soul: and all that is within me, bless his holy name" (Ps. 103:1 RSV).

Teachers are witnessing to their faith in God.

One reporter asked the president on the telephone how this revival began. He responded, "It is just as though Jesus walked in and He has been here ever since."

A witness: "For every prayer He answered, He gave me two more burdens. You should see my prayer list now."

10:30 P.M. "And Can It Be." Forty-two souls at the altar. I have just seen a couple arise from the altar after three and one-half hours of prayer. They are victorious.

The laying on of hands at the altar. Intense sobbing at one end of the altar.

Very softly we are singing "My Jesus I Love Thee."—More memories—A long time has passed since I first heard God speak to me through this song. Be patient and wait for God.

A lovely young lady just walked to the microphone a few moments ago and said, "For the glory of God" and then she sang so

beautifully "The Battle Hymn." I wish you could have heard it, especially when 1,500 other voices sang in the night. O how glorious. Hands outstretched in the air . . . overwhelming. I am simply overcome with the joy of this moment.

A mother and father are rejoicing over a wayward college son who has just knelt at the altar. How beautiful to see this family at the altar.

An urgent need for missionaries. Incredible need. Near midnight. I see a girl in the very last seat, high in the balcony. Her head is bowed low in a deep spirit of prayer. Serenity—Peace— The answer to the needs of the world. An utter peace. The peace of God which passeth all understanding.

Father, each one of your children has a different personality. Help me.
Prayers for an alcoholic in Lexington. "Great Is Thy Faithfulness." Prayers for a youth retreat in New York State. Some people are waiting well over an hour to witness.

Midnight has just come and gone. Nineteen at the altar. "Whiter Than Snow."
John 12:32. "When I Survey."
12:45 A.M. and a new day.

February 7, 1970 8:20 A.M. on this Saturday morning. The altar is flooded with seekers.
Prayers for the administration. The professors.
A witness: "Keep on Keeping on."
Beautiful singing. Over a thousand here on this winter morning.

"The Heavens declare the Glory of God."

8:40 A.M. The president is urging a long view of these days we have spent in the presence of God. He speaks to us out of the fifty-fifth chapter of Isaiah, beginning with the first verse. "Ho, every one who thirsts, come to the waters; and he who has no money, come, buy and eat!" Here we see not the struggle of man, but we see a very clear and beautiful invitation from God.

In these past days there is a sense in which God has separated us from the world and shut the world out so that He could speak. God has our attention.

God wants us. We are involved in a purpose. A mission. We must be a flying wedge in a pagan society. God wants to get us ready. What is God getting us ready for? Let us walk seriously, meekly, obediently.

Ninety-five hours have passed. Last night when we sang "The Battle Hymn" it was a heavenly moment. But, how infinitely more beautiful will be our situation in Heaven as we sing around the Throne of God.

The most wonderful thing in life is to be used of God.

For ninety-six hours now, God has been moving. God makes things real to us through His Spirit. The urgency of meeting God.

Students from other colleges in this section of our nation are here. I see a whole group of students from a visiting college as they weep for revival on their campus.

40

So hard to let go of pride. "O how I love Him, how I adore Him."

A witness: "Christ has begun to work in my heart in His fullness."

4:05 P.M. Three hundred–four hundred people are here in Hughes. Many visitors. "Tis So Sweet To Trust in Jesus"—Trust—Faith—The keys.

Witness: "I sat in Hughes last night and just let Jesus love me."

Ephesians 1:19. The immeasurable power of God. 5 souls at the altar. Visitors from Georgia and surrounding states.

He is showing me not only what He is, but what I am as His child.

"Just As I Am" 4:40 P.M. Visitors from Ohio, Rhode Island, and New Jersey. God does not tire of us coming to him in prayer. *So many hundreds of prayers have been lifted from Hughes this week.*

Many are coming tonight from various states. On our knees is the only place we need to be. Stand in awe. We are not concerned with showing people where Asbury is, but we are concerned with showing people the Christ served by Asburians. In a dying and lost world we must go.

A professor from the University of Kentucky is witnessing. Are we walking in the Spirit moment by moment?

8 P.M. Hebrews 12: verse 29, "For our God is a consuming fire." verse 6, verse 1—John 8:36—FREE INDEED—A steady stream of people going to the altar. . . . Seven people waiting to witness. "No One Ever Cared For Me Like Jesus." Thanks from an Indonesian student for American missionaries.

106 hours have passed. A report of glorious victory. "When we all get to Heaven what a day of rejoicing that will be. When we all see Jesus, we'll sing and shout the victory."

11:15 P.M. 700–800 people in Hughes. I don't know that I've ever seen the altar area so crowded.

(As Saturday faded into Sunday, I remember the singing from Hughes Auditorium. "All Hail The Power of Jesus' Name"—*HE IS BEING CROWNED. HALLELUJAH!*)

February 8, 1970 12:30 P.M. A great crowd at the altar. I saw a beautiful sight a few moments ago when an entire family made their way to the altar. I see a man who drove all the way from New Jersey at the altar. All is well.

There is a very Holy atmosphere here.

Witness: "I'm free from all the limitations I've placed on myself." Another: "Christianity doesn't get old. It gets newer each day."

"It's real." Divisions and walls have fallen. God cannot work very well until we are honest with Him. Hebrews 4:9 and "perfect rest." "Grace That Is Greater Than All Our Sins." "Grace, grace, God's grace." Marvelous Grace.

8:40 P.M. The revival goes on and on and on. Thirteen souls at the altar. 1,500–1,600 people present here in Hughes. People from many states.

"Sweep over my spirit forever, I pray, In fathomless billows of love." Indeed God has been doing just that since Tuesday morning at ten o'clock.

TO GOD BE THE GLORY. GREAT THINGS HE HAS DONE.

"That which we have seen and heard declare we unto you, that you also may have fellowship with us" (I John 1:3 KJV).

3
Out of the Heart

ARTHUR L. LINDSAY

The message of the revival has come out of the heart. Person after person has spoken in simple terms of what God has been doing in his or her life. They have spoken fearfully yet joyfully, quietly though triumphantly, with tears and smiles, but always with conviction and sincerity. Listening to them, one can hear deep theological truths framed in personal reality.

Utter honesty has been the standard. From the beginning, persons have laid their hearts bare. Unashamed of new-found peace with God, they have shared pointedly what their difficulties have been and what Jesus Christ has done to bring about a transformation.

There were some, like the youth trying to find meaning in his life, who had practically no Christian background. After the magnetism of Christ had drawn him to his knees, he testified, "I don't even know why I came to this revival, but I'm glad I did. I wish everyone could come. I had taken trips on everything before coming here to college—drugs, sex, booze, gambling, everything. I was smoking joints [*marijuana*] like they were going out of style. With drugs, you get high and then come down hard. With Christ I am going to stay on an even keel and try to get all my friends to do the same."

Most of those who experienced the touch of God were already

identified with the church. Yet despite their religious training and profession, many had never really come to know God in a personal relationship. Revealing one of the big problems, a student said, "I spent three years here totally disillusioned because I looked at Christians and not Christ. I found that if you look at Christians you are going to be let down because they're only people. And for the first time in my life I can say that I have looked at Jesus Christ. I have not been disillusioned. I have not been let down. It is the biggest thing that has ever happened to me."

One young man, son of a well-known preacher, said that he had heard thousands of sermons on the subject of salvation, but had never been saved himself. "For years I had everybody fooled, but I never really fooled myself because God gave me no peace. Now He has met the longing of my heart."

More numerous were the testimonies of those who confessed to losing the sacredness of fellowship with God. A quiet, unassuming psychology professor stunned the chapel when he brokenheartedly confessed that he had been living a sham for six years. "I have been keeping up the outward appearances, but there has been no peace or joy in my life. It has been dry. I can't go on like this." No one made a sound as he walked off the platform to the altar of prayer. But there was great rejoicing when, two days later, he reported, "God has given me a new joy in my life, a new purpose for living."

Among the hundreds of students who told of getting fed up with pretense was the editor of the student newspaper. Busy with a term paper, he had skipped the chapel on February 3. When he heard that the service was still going on, he wandered over after lunch and, as he put it, "hid my skeptical self in a corner." But he soon discovered that the Spirit of God is not limited by corners. "I knew things in my life were a lie. I was a National Merit Scholar and a real 'campus leader.' A lot of good they were doing me because I was sick and a miserably lonely young man. Yet I sat there for two hours refusing to do anything about it. A girl on my staff came up and hugged me around the neck and apologized for 'being mean' to me. That really got me, because it was I who had mistreated her!

"As I watched and listened to my fellow students, I was troubled to realize I lacked a certain joy and happiness that so many of them expressed so freely. There came that critical moment when I was forced to admit that my self-sufficiency was failing me and that I needed to be dependent upon Jesus Christ. I prayed at the altar for an hour and a half, not shedding a tear, but undergoing a spiritual revitalization that has revolutionized my life.

"There is a calmness and a certainty to life when Jesus comes. No, not all of my problems were solved immediately. What did happen was that I acquired in Christ a new resource—a greater capacity to handle my problems. I cannot overestimate the value of a renewed dedication to Christ in terms of purpose for life. What has been the greatest practical residue of the revival for me is the order and direction and power of a Christ-centered life.

"In May I became engaged to a lovely young lady whom I had dated off and on for two years. Without the revival in both of our hearts, I doubt we would be able to make the sort of commitment or share the kind of love that makes a Christian marriage. Since I have considered what marriage means in terms of giving up *me* to become part of *us,* I have been able to understand as never before the Biblical idea of Christ's marriage to the believers. As I desire to give my partner the best there is of me, so must I desire to give Christ my best. This realization has been one of the greatest spiritual experiences of my life."

Typical of hundreds of students was the testimony of a senior premedical major who testified to a new understanding of an already existing relationship with Jesus Christ. "I had been a Christian for nearly ten years, but the real freedom to express myself was never a reality in my life.

"I guess the problem was a matter of not really having accepted the forgiveness of God for the sins which I had committed. God had forgiven me all right but I had never forgiven myself.

"For years, then, I suffered under the awful burden of self-imposed, false guilt. I continually berated myself for not living up to the way of God. But in actuality I was trying to attain some high standard, which, although commendable, was artificial.

"Because of this inner restlessness I was unable in all of those years to give a meaningful verbal witness to my faith in Jesus Christ. I loved Him, and I felt led to prepare to serve Him as a missionary doctor. But I never led one person to Christ.

"But late one night in the balcony of Hughes Auditorium, feeling so worthless watching everyone come alive in the spirit of the revival, I poured out the distress of my heart to a friend. With love and understanding he helped me to see that I had been falsely punishing myself for all of these years.

"My heart began to beat with a fresh thrill as I saw that indeed God's forgiveness had afforded peace to me years before. I prayed then with joy and triumph. That seat in the balcony became a hallowed place of prayer.

"Christ has given me fresh assurance that I am His and He is mine. Although my devotion to Him in the past was fruitless, He encouraged me to begin anew. I began taking every opportunity to witness for Him.

"From the very first weekend of the revival Christ has been able to use me. That weekend in my home church two dozen people responded to an invitation to the altar after I had given my testimony. It was a new thrill to have been used of God for the first time in my life. Since then I have seized upon every chance to bear witness to my newly understood faith. I have seen hundreds of people come to know Jesus Christ."

Revival gave to many Christians a depth of love previously unknown. Not uncommon was the testimony of this college senior:

"I have struggled with the problem of the genuine reality of a Christian experience for several years. I have been emotionally uplifted and psychologically stimulated in a religious context in the past, and I could never say that these experiences were not of God. But through my inability to comprehend and unwillingness to receive, the living and factual Spirit of Christ was not completely communicated through them as a life-changing reality.

"But today I know. I know because Jesus came into my heart in the fulness of His love and met the deepest need of my life. Jesus Christ loved me when I came to Him, and that was my deepest need—to be loved."

Many of the testimonies reflected an inner struggle with the self-centered nature of man. One of the young men on campus told this story: "I have never doubted there is a God, for this fact has been taught to me all my life. At home the name and blood of Jesus Christ were always commonplace topics of discussion.

"I found early in life, however, that I could accomplish most any task that I set out to do. This caused a real ego problem in my life, resulting in a false sense of security. Even through my first three and a half years in college my ego continued to grow and the reason for 99 percent of the activities I engaged in was myself, or my need for esteem. In other words, I was my own motivation for living. Even when I would occasionally pray, there was a selfish motive behind the prayer.

"Basically, though, I was a very lonely and unsatisfied individual. Inner conflicts had me so uptight that I could not really surrender myself to God. But then came the revival.

"I was so out of it that I immediately turned it off, categorizing (as usual) all those who gave testimonies as 'insecure' people. I wondered why they couldn't work out their problems on their own instead of having to run to God all the time. So at noon I left the 'holy rollers' and enjoyed a hearty meal instead.

"Yet I went back to check the place out. Five times I returned to the auditorium and each time I became more impressed with the depth of genuineness of the meeting. The fourth time I returned I felt a tugging inside, telling me to let go of myself completely and give myself to God. Of course, I fought this, because I was so ego-involved and didn't see why I needed Him anyway. I was successful at things in which I wanted to succeed.

"I left the auditorium and walked to my dormitory where I shared with a friend my desire to let go of myself because I was so sick of being selfish and ego-centered. I also related to him, however, my fear of losing all that I had developed and worked for for so many years, especially my last three years of college.

"Twenty minutes later I found myself in the lobby of the auditorium and again I felt this special force or tugging. I began to sweat and feel very uncomfortable inside. Suddenly I found myself walking down to the altar.

"As I knelt I begged God for forgiveness for my many sins and I told Him that I wasn't going to arise until I felt assured that He had totally taken control of and changed my life. No great emotion swept me. I wasn't struck by lightning, but suddenly I felt a peace inside which I had never experienced before. I found Christ all-sufficient for each of my needs. He even took control of my superego.

"It was His transformation in the ego area of my life that surprised me most. I found that He did not strip me of my basic personality. I was still living, but it was no longer the ego-I, rather it was and is Christ living in me.

"I still had the everyday problems that I had faced before; still had the desire that had always confronted me; still had an ego. The only difference was that Christ was in control.

"I no longer have to do things to make me happy. I am able to enjoy an abiding happiness because Someone else, who is able to do so much more with my life than I could, is in charge.

"After my experience with the infilling of God's Holy Spirit, I saw every type of personality on our campus touched and caused to respond. I can't explain the open feeling that began to exist. People were actually loving one another. I too began to learn that I couldn't love anyone with my own strength, but rather I must allow Jesus to love through me. I was never before concerned for the individual, but suddenly I was filled with a yearning for others to find what I had found.

"The actual experience that I had was tremendous, but someone reminded me that I had simply taken the first step and it wasn't how I jumped, but rather how I walked when I came down. So, I realized that the whole Christian life is a 'walk', as we walk we grow.

"I was eager to begin to walk and to begin to grow. I had an immediate desire to share with others my new-found faith. I began to grow and was anxious to stick my neck out for God. I wholeheartedly volunteered to go out as often as possible as a witness for Christ. Each time the results were fantastic.

"In all of these opportunities I could hardly believe that I was actually involved in something so completely spiritual; but I had found something true and real and thrilling to challenge my total being.

"I have found that Christ gives us as much as we want and are willing to accept in the area of spiritual growth. It just depends on how far out on the limb we are willing to go for Him. I have learned, also, that God will never let us down. He wants only the best for us."

Another senior student, respected for his spiritual leadership on campus, told how he came to the realization of this same fulness of divine grace.

"Like many other students at Asbury I had been praying for revival, but had little faith that anything like this would ever take place. When it came, I should have been rejoicing in the presence of God. But my conscience was heavy. God was dealing with me, and at first I did not know why. After spending much time in prayer and introspection, I realized my true inward condition by the faithfulness of the Holy Spirit.

"The Lord had saved me from a life of sin and rebellion against Him my junior year in high school. Since that time, even though my purpose to serve God had remained true, my Christian experience had been quite unstable. I had long heard the doctrine of entire sanctification preached clearly and explicitly. There was no doubt in my mind that this work of grace subsequent to conversion was possible. To me it was evident that if I was ever going to amount to anything at all for God, I must obtain whatever it was that changed Peter on the day of Pentecost from the vacillating character he was into a vessel fit for the Master's work. Reality was what I wanted more than anything else.

"When I arose on Friday, I felt something different was going to happen. My spirit was so heavy and hungry, I knew that for me things had to come to a climax. That afternoon as I lay on my bed, my faith somehow caught hold and the Holy Spirit came in His fulness. Those moments are almost too sacred and beautiful to describe. Even after the intensity of God's marvelous revelation has diminished, the experience of heart purity remains a reality in my life."

A prominent pastor's wife shared in depth the heart struggle that she had gone through for years, and concluded, "Several months ago I put a sign above my typewriter where I work which reads, EXPECT A MIRACLE. And I said, 'Lord, I'm going to trust You to work a miracle in my life. And I'm going to go along with You in whatever direction it takes.'

"I'm here to tell you that He really has! On Thursday night a girl with whom my husband had been counseling for seven years came to me and started pouring her heart out to me. I knew that she was having a terrible struggle in her life between the powers of good and evil. So I started witnessing to her, trying to help her.

52

I finally took her to my husband to pray and she got a real victory.

"But I got a real victory too! Because God showed me how awfully short I had been selling my husband and the people of the church and the young people. I said, 'Lord, I'm not going to sell You short anymore. I'm not going to sell my husband short. I'm going out whole hog for You.'

"And that's just the way I feel. I'm a new person. My husband told me many times, 'Someday you're going to have the blessing and someday you are going to have this victory in your life.' And I just thank God that He has given me this wonderful victory after so many years of a heart that has been dried up. I thank Him for His steadfast love."

Needless to say, not everybody who testified to a new beginning has maintained the glow. Probably some were swept into the revival current on the wave of emotional sentimentality and never really came to grips with their need and the grace of God. Others may not have learned the discipline of spiritual growth.

But most of those who witnessed to personal renewal have gone on with the Lord. The best is yet to come. As one Malaysian student wrote during the summer, "For me the greatest thing about this revival lies not in the fervency of that week in February, but rather in the unfolding of God's plan in our lives now and in the years ahead. We have caught a vision. Our hearts are burdened with compassion as we see our generation living in a meaningless vacuum. We are moved to proclaim the love of God."

Such testimonies have not ended. They never will. A great chain reaction has taken place so that one witness becomes two, and those two multiply into four, and on and on.

It has been beautiful to hear men and women of all ages and walks of life give voice to what God has done and is doing in their lives. But it has been far more thrilling to watch changed lives unfold like new blossoms.

53

". . . they were all filled with the Holy Spirit, and they spoke the word of God with boldness" (Acts 4:31 RSV).

4

Campus Demonstrations

HENRY C. JAMES

The movement of God at Asbury caused persons to cherish the same thing for others. From time to time this would be heard in testimonies, and increasingly it found expression in prayer. Likewise, as news of the revival spread, people from other schools called to solicit prayer for their colleges. Faithfully these requests were shared by the congregation, and everyone joined in fervent intercession.

Before long, appeals began coming from other campuses for Asbury students to come and tell the story. This intensified the burden of prayer even as it heightened anticipation of what God was going to do. There was a sense, too, in which everyone felt personally involved in the ministry of those who went forth.

With the dispatch of these witnesses, the local revival began to take on the dimensions of a national movement. By the summer of 1970 at least 130 colleges, seminaries and Bible schools had been touched by the revival outreach, and witnesses continue to go to other schools and local churches.

The students' approach was simple, yet powerful. They described the details of the revival story and witnessed to a fresh, personal encounter with God. They told how God had delivered them from their hang-ups and "turned them on." Their witness had the ring of reality. Under the annointing of the Holy Spirit, their words became like spiritual darts which pierced the hearts and minds of many listeners.

One of the first schools to feel the impact was Azusa Pacific College near Los Angeles, California. The dean of the faculty called the president in Wichita, Kansas, and reported to him that a moving of the Holy Spirit had begun in unusual power that day at Asbury. They decided on the phone to have a student flown to their campus.

That night the Azusa faculty engaged in an all-night prayer meeting. The revival, which had already begun, "broke out in terrific power" the next morning in chapel following the testimony of the visiting Asburian.

At 11:15 A.M. on February 6 the Valley Campus looked as though it had been evacuated. Buses that normally carried loads of students to the Hillside Campus for the class period after chapel stood driverless and empty. No one strolled down the wide walkway in front of the Turner Campus Center, and no signs of life could be seen around the Marshburn Library. The usually crowded and noisy Cougar Den snack shop was quiet and dark. Upstairs, however, where over 800 members of the faculty and student body had assembled, the scene was vastly different.

The large chapel area was unusually quiet for each person in attendance was considering the impact of the message they had just heard. The speaker of the morning did not preach, but simply told what had happened at Asbury College, and shared how his own life had been affected.

Following the report, the dean of students stood and gently asked if there were "those in the audience who would like to add depth to their religious experience by getting closer to God." He asked any such individual to step to the front of the chapel. At that moment, 150 students stepped out en masse, moved to the front, and made altars out of chairs. This mighty surge of the Holy Spirit brought confessions, tears, restitutions and cleansing power.

After a time of prayer those who had made decisions stood up to testify about their experiences. One girl said, "I poured out my heart to God." Another young lady stated, "I have been playing a game with God to see how much of my life I could keep. Now that game is over, I belong to Him." A boy spoke out saying, "Jesus is real; He is the answer."

Afternoon classes for the day were cancelled and numbers of students stayed to hear the testimonies, pray, and sing for over seven hours. Later, smaller prayer groups met in dormitory rooms and in classrooms. Others left the campus to go to nearby colleges to share the good news. Students began telephoning their parents and pastors across the country to tell them about the wonderful experience that had occurred.

After the seven-hour chapel service on Friday, the students used the half-time of the basketball game that night to witness to the people from the community who had come to the game. More unusual, and particularly strange to the opposing players, when the Azusa team made a basket, students sometimes were heard to shout, "Praise the Lord!" Following the game several hundred students met again in the auditorium for another two-hour session of witnessing, praise, and Holy Communion.

The next Sunday many students related the same experiences to congregations where they were members. In several instances pastors did not preach prepared sermons because people wanted to renew their relationships with Christ right then and there. So the revival broke out in many churches.

One student called on the Sirhan home in the Los Angeles area.

For an hour-and-a-half he shared with the mother and brother of Robert Kennedy's assassin about the love of Christ.

The following Monday at the regular chapel period, students began sharing with each other the many events that had transpired over the weekend. The witness continued when afternoon classes were cancelled. For hours, the testimonies and singing went on. Students gave credit to God for the way the Holy Spirit had worked in their lives and in the lives of others.

One student spoke of the spiritual touch in his own life: "Some will think tomorrow will be the same, but it won't be. Tomorrow will be different!" This was an accurate prediction. The next day the chaplain at Azusa took ten students to Pasadena College where some of them shared with the student body. Those who were interested in praying for a revival and hearing more of the student witnesses were invited to remain after the benediction. About 150 students and faculty members remained to hear the rest of the students.

Then the Pasadena College basketball coach came to the microphone and in a voice filled with emotion said, "I have not been the Christian witness I should have been in front of the men on the team. I have failed them as a Christian. I want God to forgive me. I am a different person." The effect was like an electric shock and the pattern of revival started all over again, this time on the Pasadena campus. Students began to come forward and confess their hostility toward others, their hypocrisy on campus, and the work of forgiveness which had been done in their hearts.

The chapel continued for two or three more hours, and a prayer meeting that night continued the witnessing. Immediately several prayer groups which had been formed two weeks previously to pray for revival began to swell. Some groups which had struggled to persuade five or six to attend now jumped to seventy-five and more in the dorm lounges. The spirit of revival began to move out across the campus.

Greenville College in Greenville, Illinois, was another school to be shaken. One professor noted in retrospect that for several weeks prior to the revival, the Holy Spirit noticeably had been working with some persons on the campus. Here and there, individuals had been led to face their spiritual needs and to experience God's forgiveness and wholeness.

Soon after the revival broke at Asbury Seminary, a student who was an alumnus of Greenville stood in one of the services and expressed a burden for his alma mater. He told of some of the tensions on campus; then, asking for united prayer, he broke down and wept. Moments later a local pastor stood and announced that a request for a witness team had just been received from Greenville. Immediately the graduates from this college attending the seminary gathered around the altar to pray. When they arose from their knees, a delegation was selected, and within a half-hour they were on their way.

After a hard night's drive through sleet and snow, the nine seminarians and one collegian arrived at Greenville. The next morning in chapel they shared their witness. Immediately, "as though a great barrier had burst," students began to seek the Lord "for every sort of personal and spiritual need." Individuals began to confess publicly their wrong attitudes, to witness to a personal wholeness and the new thing that the Holy Spirit was doing in them and through them.

An atmosphere of prayer, witnessing, and of general spiritual freedom continued among persons in the college church sanctuary until the early morning hours of Saturday. Many students and faculty members left the campus to witness to home church congregations. Others shared their new faith with students who had chosen to remain skeptical.

A service Wednesday night brought together a large gathering of expectant students, faculty and visiting ministers. Such a magnificent visitation of the Holy Spirit resulted that over 200 persons were still present, seeking Christ, repenting, asking and receiving forgiveness from other persons at 2:30 A.M. That service continued until 5 A.M.

Later, the campus coordinator wrote: "Greenville College will never be the same. The Holy Spirit has blown in gale force through our dorms and classrooms, our faculty and administrative offices and has settled like a heavenly cloud over the sanctuary of the college church . . . Teams of students and faculty have been fanning out over the Midwest in weekends of witnessing and the reports read like the Book of Acts."

Later, when Terry Dickson, a reporter for the *St. Louis Post-Dispatch,* visited the campus to check out a news story, he was surprised to learn that the students did not want to talk about Cambodia or racial injustice, though they were deeply concerned about these problems. He wrote this in a May 24 report:

They wanted to talk about what happened to them when they were caught up in a spiritual upheaval that turned the whole college upside down, so to speak, and changed their lives forever. There was nothing pietistic in their attitudes. They were open, friendly, smiling, bright-eyed and as eager to tell about it as students at another college would be to tell about how they won the Big Game. Which, in a sense, they felt they had done.

Not surprisingly, calls came from other places for students to come and share with them. Teams went to Central and Miltonvale (Kansas) Colleges, and the same scenes of revival followed. One group went to Millikin (Illinois) University to spread the word. In the student union they were joined by many Millikin students and they formed a circle and joined hands. When some black students started jeering and heckling, the students just opened the circle, took the blacks by the hand and said, "What's with you?" and then drew them in. This was more than the hecklers expected. "They were bombed out," as one of the Greenville group put it. "They wanted to talk to us, they wanted to find what we had found," reporter Dickson wrote about the incident.

Leaders of the Free Methodist Church testify that as a result of the numerous witness teams going out from Greenville College, the majority of their churches in the Wabash, Southern Michigan, and Central Illinois Conferences have been revitalized, and the entire spiritual tone of these conferences has been transformed.

News of the Asbury revival reached Southwestern Baptist Theological Seminary in Fort Worth, Texas, where for two years some students and faculty had been praying for a movement of God on their campus.

When the Kentucky awakening was reported to one class by a professor, "spontaneously the entire group fell before the Lord in prayer—confessions, bold intercessions, compassionate pleas for personal and seminary revival poured forth with beautiful liberty." Another professor shared the revival news with his class, and the same thing happened. The whole period was spent in earnest supplication before the Lord. When the bell rang for dismissal of the class, one student ran down the hall to report to one of his teachers. He was carrying his glasses in his hand, his face was bathed with tears, radiant joy was written on his face and victory came through his voice as he said, "You know that revival we have been praying for? I believe it is already here!" (Most of the information contained in this section is taken from a paper on the revival written by Dr. Jack Gray, Professor of Missions at South-

61

western Baptist Theological Seminary. We are grateful for permission to quote from this manuscript.)

An invitation was extended for some Asbury students to come and report firsthand about their experiences. One of those students who went with the witness team recalled how they "prayed all the way to Texas." When they arrived on campus they walked into a prayer meeting in the student center where forty to fifty students were gathered. They were confessing sins, asking for forgiveness and requesting prayer for each other. One of the students told how he had contemplated suicide, but had found the answer in Christ. The revival was already well under way.

Arrangements had been made for the Asbury students to occupy pulpits in the area on Sunday. A marked spirit of revival was felt in the services, with scores of people evidencing renewal in their lives. Many people openly admitted a wide variety of sins and animosities and sought to restore broken relationships.

A special service in the Scarborough Preaching Chapel at Southwestern Baptist Seminary on Monday was announced for 4 P.M. The Asbury students shared for about fifteen minutes, then sat down. There was an awkward silence for a moment, then a young preacher arose, and with measured deliberation, began to confess the deep needs of his heart. Then another student arose, and another. Student after student confessed resentment, bitterness, lust, jealousy and cheating.

In describing the service, Dr. Gray gave this account:

One young wife arose and haltingly, but with determination to complete what she had stood to her feet to do, said, "I was born and reared in a preacher's home. Now I am married to a preacher. I've gone to church all of my life just because it was the thing to do. But it has never meant much to me. Now I know why. I've just asked Jesus to come into my heart, and He has." Joy sparkled in her tears as she sat down, converted on the spot!

A young man, due to graduate in less than two months, came to the pulpit stand; agony had distorted his countenance. He poured out his confession of a habit of dishonesty in his studies. "This is eating me up!" he sobbed. "I've got to get rid of it—pray for me." He sank to his knees right there and claimed the cleansing of the Lord.

Trying to describe the atmosphere of this service, one who was there said, "God was declaring His presence and demanding an audience with each of us. At times even though we were in the crowd we felt ourselves closeted with Him, and we experienced both the honor and the hurt of His private dealings with us. It was awesome. We knew what we were seeing, hearing, feeling, and thinking was not the product of our imaginations. We were meeting God in all His majesty."

The meeting went on until the early hours of the morning. When the crowd at last dispersed, meetings with the Lord continued in homes, dorm rooms and parlors. All through the night students at odds with each other met in sweet reconciliation.

The next day the Asbury witnesses spoke in individual and combined classes. Again students were moved to make confessions and ask forgiveness. Following a time of sharing at a 3 P.M. service more students found the joy and victory of a clean heart.

That evening a meeting had been called in the dormitories to ratify a new school constitution. But attention in the meetings soon turned to revival. In one dorm the hallway and stairway became cluttered where students had gathered to witness and pray. Confessions, restitutions, hugging and praising God were the pattern until 1:30 A.M., with some students continuing to seek God through the night.

The next morning following a Founder's Day observance students who desired to hear more about the revival were invited to remain in the chapel. Only a dozen or so left, while twelve hundred stayed to hear the witnesses. God moved again upon hearts in a sweet, penetrating way.

Commenting on the movement of the Spirit during those days, a professor writes: "The long-awaited renewal was here! Not all of the seminary had opportunity to share, but more profound work of graphic encounter with God had taken place than some of us knew to expect. Through the rest of the week we found ourselves walking in a sense of reverent awe, our minds racing with questions, our wills painfully adjusting to the demands of what God had wrought, our hearts reaching out in eager desire to tell others, and our souls lifted in glorious joy, praise, and new dimensions of loving adoration of the Lord."

Olivet Nazarene College located in Kankakee, Illinois, was another school to feel the impact of revival. According to one observer, the college "came unglued" as two students from Asbury witnessed on campus. The president was quoted in the Kankakee *Daily Journal*, a local newspaper, "I've seen nothing to compare with it in my twenty-one years as president."

A scheduled speaker was unable to appear for chapel and the pastor asked several students to give personal testimonies. Students began leaving their classes and by late morning nearly everyone on campus was at Chalfant Hall either giving themselves to God or praying as others did so.

Hundreds of Olivet students moved out to tell their story with the result that revival fires were kindled in many other places. One student went to the Nazarene Theological Seminary in Kansas City, Missouri. As he was describing his experience, one of the seminary students started to the altar "weeping so strongly that he could scarcely see where he was going; he bumped into the piano, spun off and finally knelt at the communion rail," reported *The Seminary Tower,* a Nazarene publication. The students from Olivet continued to share as others came until the altar was filled with weeping students.

What was described by one reporter as "an all night religious sit-in" developed at Georgetown College near Lexington, Kentucky, after six Asbury students gave their testimony at an evening vesper service. Throughout the night students shared their experiences, sang songs of faith and love, and joined in prayer. So large was the crowd that the students requested permission to use the college chapel for the meeting. They were reminded that a rehearsal for a forthcoming religious emphasis week was already scheduled for the night. "But why do you wish to prepare for religious emphasis next week when you can have it now," queried the students. Accordingly the director called off the practice, and with some of the college administration and faculty, joined nearly 700 students in the marathon revival. Both the *Lexington Leader* and the Louisville *Courier-Journal* gave accounts of this revival.

Other stories of revival could be told of Houghton (N.Y.), Wheaton (Ill.), Oral Roberts (Okla.), Trevecca (Tenn.), John Wesley (N.C.), Berea (Ky.), Marion (Ind.), Huntington (Ind.), George Carver (Georgia), Canadian Bible (Sask.), Seattle Pacific (Wash.), Fort Wayne (Ind.), St. Paul (Minn.), Central Wesleyan (S.C.), Taylor (Ind.), Eastern Mennonite (Va.), Spring Arbor (Mich.), Canadian Nazarene (Manitoba), Union University (Tenn.), Oklahoma Baptist, Roberts Wesleyan (N.Y.), Weyland Baptist (Tex.), Sue Bennett (Ky.), Grace (Ind.), George Fox (Ore.), Fuller Seminary (Calif.), to mention only a few. Each school had its own version, and the extent of penetration varied. But in all the pattern was marked by a contagious spirit of honest witnessing.

To date, the movement has centered in Christian schools. However, the revival has had an outreach on the campuses of some large secular universities. A number of students from the University of Kentucky visited Asbury during the spontaneous revival in February, and a few were converted. These students and others from Asbury have carried their personal witness to the nearby university, as well as other state campuses. One group of witnesses saw numbers of students moved to seek God at Western Kentucky State University.

Meetings for witnessing have been arranged in many different ways. A prominent member of the faculty at the University of Tennessee at Martin invited four students to share their testimony at a meeting which he sponsored. Two hundred decisions were recorded. Thereafter, until commencement, scores of Tennessee students met every night in the dormitories for prayer. At the University of Delaware, a group of evangelical students pooled their resources to have six Asburians fly to their campus with the news of what God was doing. Through the Baptist Student Movement the Asbury story was told at Texas A. & M. and the University of Texas at Arlington, as well as the five largest state universities in Oklahoma. Sometimes the meetings of confession lasted four or five hours with hundreds of students making new commitments to Christ.

As yet there does not appear to be a spiritual breakthrough at all levels of any large secular university, but the possibility exists in spite of the difficulties. Such organizations as the Campus Crusade for Christ, Inter-Varsity Christian Fellowship, the Navigators, Fellowship of Christian Athletes, along with some warmhearted church witnessing groups, already are having a tremendous impact on many campuses.

If revival could spread into the inner life of our large universities, as well as many of the smaller church-supported schools, the change that would ensue in our nation is staggering to contemplate. Billy Graham in his "Hour of Decision" broadcast on March 15 expressed the burden felt by many when he said, "It is my prayer that Christians throughout the world will be praying that the spiritual refreshment which started at Asbury College in Kentucky will sweep from campus to campus and from city to city."

". . . you shall receive power, when the Holy Spirit has come upon you, and you shall be my witnesses . . ." (Acts 1:8 RSV).

5

Churches Come Alive

JOHN T. SEAMANDS

As news of the Asbury revival spread across the country, hundreds of pastors began requesting student teams to come and share the story with the members of their congregations. Every Saturday for the next several months, a large procession of cars left Wilmore, headed for all points of the compass. Many students traveled by air to distant assignments.

Almost invariably, wherever the witness teams went, the results were the same. Pastor and people responded. The sermon and order of service were pushed aside for the moment. Many church members, tired of pretending for so long, took off their masks and exposed their own hypocrisy and phoniness. Broken in spirit, they openly confessed their needs, prayed and shared with one another. Church altars which for years had been nothing more than pieces of furniture now became hallowed places where men met God and brother was reconciled to brother. The usual stiffness and formality gave way to a new freedom in the Spirit. With hearts full of joy, members of the congregation lifted their hands in the air and sang forth the praises of God. People paid no attention to the clock; they forgot about food. They sat for hours in the sanctuary, basking in the presence of God.

In many instances, the students' testimonies sparked an unusual, spontaneous revival that lasted for days and influenced the entire community. Such was the case in Anderson, Indiana, where a marvelous "revival of love" ensued.

In the early phase of the awakening on the campus of Asbury College, three students who were members of the Church of God felt their "hearts strangely warmed." They immediately became burdened for spiritual renewal within their own denomination. After a time of prayer together, they decided to mail out news releases of the revival story to twenty pastors with whom they were acquainted.

One of the letters was sent to an alumnus of Asbury College who was pastor of the South Meridian Church of God in Anderson, Indiana. The pastor was deeply moved by the Wilmore story. At the same time, an eighty-year-old lady who was a member of his church said, "Pastor, word has reached me that revival has broken out on the campus of Asbury College. Would it be possible to invite a witness team to Anderson to share the news with our congregation?" He immediately phoned Wilmore and invited a team.

On Saturday afternoon, February 21, the Asbury witness team arrived in Anderson. The group consisted of four girls and three boys, and was led by a senior student at Asbury Seminary, an alumnus of Anderson College. They went straight to the campus of the college and mingled with students in the dormitory rooms and lounges sharing the revival news and extending invitations to the Sunday morning service.

At the 10:45 A.M. worship service in the South Meridian Church all seven members of the Asbury team gave their witness before a congregation of about five hundred. Even before an invitation was given, people started to go forward to pray at the altar. Several publicly expressed their personal spiritual needs. This was followed by a time of testimony and sharing. The service lasted almost three hours, with an unusual sense of the presence of God.

The attendance was larger at the evening service. Again the program was informal, and for the second time the Asbury team gave their witness. The response was the same. For several hours people kept filling the altar for prayer and going before the microphone to give their witness. One local college student said enthusiastically, "This is no longer the Asbury Revival. This is the Anderson Revival!" It was quite evident to all that an unusual movement of the Spirit was taking place at South Meridian Church. The people were gripped with a feeling of spiritual excitement and expectancy.

The pastor was now faced with an important decision. Should he continue the meetings? After prayerful deliberation he announced that there would be a service the next evening.

Monday evening about 1,000 people crowded into the sanctuary which ordinarily holds only 750. Many had to stand along the walls. Three church buses made ten trips back and forth from the college campus to provide transportation for the students. The Asbury team shared their witness for the last time before returning to Wilmore to resume classes.

Again the Spirit of God moved upon the entire congregation. In the balcony, little prayer groups began to form here and there. One youth leader knelt with his entire youth fellowship, and, after a period of prayer, the whole group made its way down to the altar. There were so many high school and college students crowded around the altar, that again and again the pastor had to request them gently to return to their seats and make room for others who wanted to come.

There were periodic outbursts of praise and song. A fourteen-

71

year-old student stood before the mike and said, "We've been clapping and rejoicing with one another all night. I think we should give Jesus a hand." The remark touched off a standing ovation that lasted for two or three minutes. "It was like a star coming off the basketball floor," the pastor recalled.

Following the service the pastor began to feel that the meeting was becoming too big for one man to handle. Early Tuesday morning he phoned several key businessmen and fellow pastors and invited them to meet him for breakfast in a local restaurant. About twenty men responded. Around the breakfast table they formulated plans to continue and expand the revival. Some of the laymen volunteered to place a large paid advertisement in the local newspaper and to prepare the church gymnasium for overflow crowds.

That evening the attendance swelled to around 1,400. Both the sanctuary and gym were filled. The following night, in spite of a championship basketball game in town, the sanctuary was again crowded. Several outstanding conversions took place. Among those transformed were an alcoholic, an extremely rebellious student, an outstanding athlete and a Roman Catholic. The service lasted until eleven o'clock.

By now the local news media were featuring "the Anderson revival" in their reports and articles. Revival became the talk of the town.

Noon meetings were begun in the city hall and gained momentum until as many as 200 were in regular attendance. The group included businessmen, night shift factory workers, housewives and students. Still other business and professional people were attending a daily prayer breakfast at a downtown hotel. Several Youth for Christ organizations sprang up in the public schools. High schoolers arrived at school a half hour early each day to study the Bible and pray together. Spontaneous prayer meetings were held in the college dormitories and in the homes of teachers and church members all across town.

Visitors from out of state soon began pouring into Anderson "to get a taste of the revival." They came from Kentucky, West Virginia, Illinois, Nebraska, Kansas, Canada, and as far west as California. Many came merely to observe, but experienced inward renewal and returned home with something new to share.

On Sunday afternoon, March 8, a special rally was held in the South Side Junior High gymnasium with over 2,000 people attending. At this meeting a hippie with full beard received Christ as his Saviour and bore witness before the whole congregation. An eighty-year-old grandmother, her snow-white hair done up in a bun, went forward and hugged him. Within a few days the young man had led two of his fellow musicians to the Lord, and they were all out witnessing to their friends. The following Sunday afternoon, a second city-wide rally was held in the North Side Junior High gymnasium and this time the crowd reached almost 2,600.

Soon calls were coming in from pastors in many states asking for witness teams from Anderson to come and share the revival spirit with their congregations. A special revival fund was set up and people contributed hundreds of dollars to pay the travel expenses of the team members. By the first week in May these witness teams had visited scores of churches in thirty-one states and Canada. Everywhere they went, the power of the Holy Spirit was manifest in the services and hundreds of young people and adults made commitments to Jesus Christ. One Sunday in Roanoke, Virginia, over 150 people knelt at the altar in prayer. In Huntington, West Virginia, a spontaneous revival broke out in the Trinity Church of God. Services continued for two weeks. For several Sunday mornings the attendance at the South Meridian Church in Anderson was greatly depleted, because so many of the members were out on witness assignments. With a smile the pastor remarked, "It wouldn't bother me at all, if one Sunday morning I came to conduct the worship service and no one would be present—as long as I knew my people were out sharing God's love with others."

The revival services continued in the South Meridian Church for fifty consecutive nights (February 22 to April 12) with an average attendance of about 1,000. Barriers were broken down as members of various denominations, black and white, young and old, all found a common meeting place at the foot of the cross. There was no fixed program and no formal preaching. A typical service lasted for two to three hours and consisted of singing, confession, prayer and testimony.

Those present on one Saturday night will probably never forget the confession of a man in his mid-fifties, who stood before the microphone and said, "I have been an active church member for years. I have directed many summer youth camps—but I've been a phony." Then he went on to relate how in the new reorganization of schools in the city, he had been so hostile to some members of the school board that out of spite he had placed dead skunks in their mailboxes and smeared red paint on their driveways. When the Holy Spirit convicted him of his meanness, he went to each one of the homes and confessed that he was the culprit. In one of the homes, the husband said angrily, "I threatened to shoot the man if I ever found him out." Later he mellowed and expressed admiration for the man's courage in confessing.

Many described the Anderson happening as "a revival of love." "As God's love filled our hearts," one pastor explained, "all denominational, racial and age barriers were torn down. Congregational rifts were healed, the generation gap bridged, and families reunited."

James Massey, the chaplain at Anderson College, summarized

the effects of the revival upon the college students in these carefully worded statements in the college newspaper.

The Revival is a spiritual phenomenon of integrity. This happening has given to hundreds of students an experience of genuine spiritual value. Counseling sessions with students have convinced me this happening has been deeper than mere emotion. Some students have at last entered into true and worthy commitments. Scores of others now have adopted proper standards for their lives. Christian beliefs have become important—and redemptive. The attitudes of many students have become less censorious and more meaningfully centered and controlled. I have heard many confessions that let me know that prejudices are being examined and released. The Revival has helped students to relate love to logic, feeling to facts and faith to reason.

In a front-page Sunday feature article on April 12, 1970, a *Chicago Tribune* reporter wrote about it enthusiastically.

The revival has made a splash that is sending ripples throughout the country. Nobody can recall a similar church-related event that has drawn this kind of response in Anderson. Many people who came prepared to be skeptical at the emotional nature of the meetings have been impressed with the sincerity and the contagious atmosphere of the sessions. . . . In a day when many congregations are worried about losing their appeal to young people, Anderson's "Revival of Love" seems to be saying something.

Another dramatic spiritual movement—an unusual *youth re-*

vival—was that which took place in a small county-seat town in Tennessee.

The spring vacation (March 15–22) offered the students on the Asbury campus a wonderful opportunity to scatter all across the nation and witness before innumerable congregations. They became instruments in God's hands to light revival fires in many churches.

One of the witness teams was a group of three seminary students who were invited to conduct a preaching mission at Holly Avenue United Methodist Church in South Pittsburg, Tennessee, twenty-five miles west of Chattanooga. The congregation of this church is not large, but comprises a number of professional people and leading citizens of the community.

As for the youth of South Pittsburg, they were typical of young people found across the nation today. Many are dependable and talented, while others are undisciplined and reckless, seeking their kicks in drugs, sex and car racing. The community had recently been shaken over the tragic death of a small child, the victim of a hot-rod speedster.

The mission got off to a slow start with light attendance at the Sunday services and little response from the congregation. At the close of the day, the young evangelists were visibly discouraged.

On Monday morning, however, the team had the opportunity to witness about the Asbury revival to about seven hundred students in the local high school. The young people seemed deeply impressed, and many tarried after the assembly to chat privately with the team members.

That evening the youth choir increased from fifteen members to fifty, and the church was filled with young people and adults. After the message an altar invitation was given. Thirty-six young people responded and committed their lives to Jesus Christ.

On Tuesday evening opportunity was given for witnessing.

76

Many of the new converts spoke excitedly about their new relationship with Christ. So effective was their exhortation that the sermon was omitted and an invitation extended to others who wanted to receive Christ. Again there was an unusual response.

As a result of many students witnessing in the classrooms and hallways to the saving power of Jesus Christ, the revival was now spreading to the high school. Wednesday evening the church was filled and the youth choir numbered one hundred.

At this service many key young people were won to the Lord, among them an outstanding and popular football player. A born leader, he exerted an adverse influence on many of the students. He was a restless boy, transferred from one high school to another, and finally he dropped out of school halfway through his senior year. A heavy drinker, he had spent the previous Saturday night in jail for drunk and disorderly conduct.

While many of his friends were praying and testifying around the altar, the football player slipped up to the platform, took the student leader by the arm, and led him outside the church. "I've been looking for something all my life," he said. "I think this is it, but I want to be sure it's real." As the student lovingly reassured him, he knelt on the sidewalk, confessed his sins, and accepted Christ as his personal Saviour. He immediately rushed inside to the microphone to give his witness. Through tears he confessed, "I've finally found what I've been looking for; not in all this other stuff—sex and booze and drugs—but in Christ!" Two days later he held the entire assembly of the Jasper High School spellbound, as he narrated to almost a thousand students the great change that had taken place in his life.

At the same service, an alcoholic, who had been separated from his wife for over two years, was marvelously converted and reunited with his family. Just two days previously his twelve-year-old son had received Christ and had requested the congregation to pray for his father's conversion. On this evening the father was drinking beer in a tavern eighteen miles away, when the Spirit of God convicted him and urged him to seek out his children. When he walked into the Holly Avenue Church, his son was giving his witness over the mike. For a long time he sat listening to the testimonies; finally, about eleven o'clock that night, he walked down to the altar and surrendered his life to Christ. The next evening he sat on the second row with his wife and two boys, and shared his experience with the entire congregation. Since then he has given up his part-ownership in the liquor store and has been going out on weekends, witnessing to the Saviour's love.

By Thursday the crowds had completely outgrown the capacity of the church which could seat only about three hundred. Large numbers were being turned away from the services, and many adults were purposely staying at home to make room for the youth. It was quite evident to all that another meeting-place should be sought. Knowing the situation, the Baptist minister very graciously offered his church which has a seating capacity of 750. He also contacted three of the leading black citizens in town and made it clear that the blacks were welcome.

The Friday and Saturday evening meetings were outstanding. The church was crowded with both adults and young people. There were students from the Jasper High School and visitors from out of town. Ministers of many denominations were present. Each night the service lasted until almost midnight and was characterized by periods of confession, repentance, witnessing and singing.

Saturday evening was to be the closing service of the revival, but the Asbury team was invited to stay on for the two Sunday services in the United Methodist Church. The morning service began at 11 o'clock and did not close until 2:30 in the afternoon. During the latter part of the service the local Catholic priest dropped in. The previous evening, a young man belonging to his parish had been converted at the service in the Baptist church, and had shared the news with him, so the priest came to see the revival for himself. Unable to find a seat in the sanctuary, he was forced to stand at the back for almost two hours. At the close of the service, he said to the pastor, "This is one of the finest things I have ever seen. If there is anything I can do to help, please call on me. I want to be a part of this movement."

By five o'clock that evening the church was filled again, with people sitting in the Sunday school rooms and many standing outside. The altar service and witnessing continued until past 11 P.M.

That Sunday there were scenes of revival in several churches throughout the city as many who had made commitments during the week shared their experiences in their own congregations.

The pastor's fifteen-year-old granddaughter was present at the Sunday morning service in the Holly Avenue Church. She received Christ during the service and gave a glowing witness before the congregation. That afternoon she and her family drove back to their home church (Baptist) for the evening service. After his sermon, the pastor invited the girl to come to the pulpit and give her witness. When she finished, nine people out of the small congregation came to the altar for prayer.

In this way the revival has spread to many surrounding schools and churches, as the young people of South Pittsburg have gone out to tell the good news that Jesus is able to save all. One week a group of thirty-six of these high-school students chartered a bus and came to Wilmore, Kentucky, and spent two days on the Asbury College campus, witnessing in the chapel and dormitories.

Soon after the revival, the local newspaper, *South Pittsburg Hustler*, carried this front-page headline: YOUTH REVIVAL ROCKS COMMUNITY. It was estimated that perhaps 500 out of the 700 students in the local high school had made commitments to Jesus

Christ. One pastor remarked: "Our town is a new town since the revival. Tough kids have been converted; broken homes reunited; alcoholics rehabilitated in society; and our churches revitalized. This is God's work!"

When two student pastors related the revival story in the First Baptist Church, Mableton, Georgia, there was a great response from the congregation and many came to the altar for prayer. Three young men received a call to the ministry; another a call to missionary service. One of the men went home and told his wife about his call, but she was upset. She said, "Honey, this is one time you'll have to go it alone. I'm not one of God's children and don't intend to be a minister's wife." However, she accompanied her husband to the evening service, and when the invitation was given, she went forward and surrendered herself to Christ. She then went to the microphone, confessed what she had said to her husband in the morning, and went on to say, "Now I'm a child of God and I'm on the team with my husband." The pastor said about the day's activities: "God did more in one moment, than we have done in five years!"

Eight Asbury College students went to Coalport, Pennsylvania. Great manifestations of the Spirit came to several churches, spreading into the high school where many youth were converted, along with some teachers.

Arrangements had been made for someone to speak in the small church at Stifflertown, but there were not enough students to fill this appointment. It happened that a girl from the college lived nearby, and was home for the Spring holidays. She was asked to take the assignment since no one else was available. With trepidation she went to the church and told her story. The power of God fell upon the people and revival broke out that continued for eight nights to standing room only crowds. In one service, the girl's father, afflicted with curvature of the spine since childhood, was miraculously healed. The whole community was shaken.

Thus the revival that had begun at Asbury continued its wondrous growth in church after church. On March 8, three Asbury College students flew to Denver, Colorado, at the invitation of the pastor of the famous Calvary Temple. The team shared the revival story with the members of the adult and college Sunday school classes, and briefly with the entire congregation in the morning services. In the evening, they had the opportunity of witnessing at length to an audience of 2,400. When the invitation was given, hundreds of people came forward, filling the altar four different times, as each time the seekers were directed to a separate counseling room. The service continued for five hours.

It is impossible to get an accurate account of how many churches have been influenced by the revival in the past few months. By the end of May approximately 2,000 witness teams had gone out on missions from Asbury College and Seminary. Each team ministered to several churches, sometimes as many as fifteen to twenty-five on a single trip. Multiply this by hundreds of other teams that went out from scores of church-related colleges, and this will give some indication of how far-reaching and intensive the influence has been.

Witnesses are beginning to take the revival story to fields of harvest overseas. Two seminary couples went to Colombia, South America. In ten days they spoke twenty-five times and saw the Holy Spirit work in the same manner as at Asbury. Other witnesses visited five continents of the world during the summer of 1970. The number reached may seem small by comparison to the need, but teams are still out witnessing, and this is not the end!

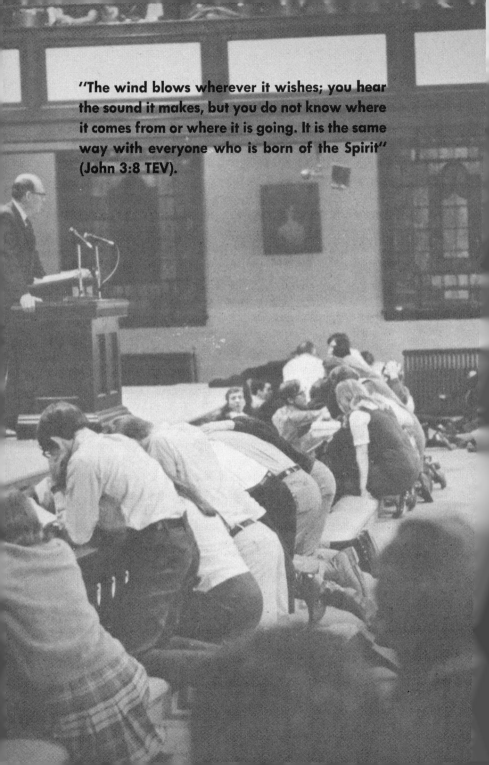

"The wind blows wherever it wishes; you hear the sound it makes, but you do not know where it comes from or where it is going. It is the same way with everyone who is born of the Spirit" (John 3:8 TEV).

6
By All Means

THOMAS A. CARRUTH

Revived persons began at once to use every means to tell the good news. Witnessing by word of mouth has been the great avenue of outreach, but by no means, though, has it been confined to colleges and churches where invitations were extended. Students have made their own opportunities to witness. One might rise from the altar, for example, and go immediately to the dormitory to seek a friend to share his experience. Some could be found witnessing on the street, going from door to door passing out tracts, talking in shopping centers, filling stations, barber shops, grocery stores, factories and places of business.

These spontaneous, on-the-spot testimonies in unexpected places have probably brought more unchurched people to consider the gospel than anything else. Hundreds of stories have been told of people finding God through these means, and new victories are reported almost every day.

One student witnessed to the president of the bank in a central Oklahoma city. The man, a nominal Christian, confessed the need in his life for real conversion and knelt in his office to accept Christ. He then called his entire staff together in the lobby of the bank for a prayer service. The Asbury student witnessed and the bank president also gave a moving witness of how Christ had become real in his life.

A group of students traveling across country on a witness team stopped in a service station because the nearby one for which they had a credit card was closed. The station was operated by a young couple married only a few months. One of the girls talked to the young wife who confessed that her love for her husband had turned out to be nothing but infatuation. She was miserable, empty, disillusioned and about to leave her husband whose deep love for her she could not reciprocate.

After witnessing to her of Christ and His love, the student asked the girl if she did not want to accept Christ who could fill her with perfect love and free her from her sin and self. The young woman bowed her head and uttered a fervent prayer of confession and asked the Lord to come into her life and cleanse her. "I feel so clean! so clean!" she exclaimed. Then she prayed for God to take away her unwillingness to love her husband.

While the two girls talked, one of the fellows witnessed to the husband between customers. After his wife told him of her experience with Christ and of the love He had given her for him, the young man also received Christ. Three and a half hours after stopping for gas the witness team left two happy young people united through Christ to each other in a genuine love. Revival had come to a Georgia garage.

A long bench in the Fulton County jail in Atlanta became a tear-drenched altar one Sunday afternoon in March as an Asbury Seminary student witnessed to the inmates of God's moving in the revival. Eighty of the 89 male prisoners, all under thirty years of age, responded with a confession of faith in Jesus Christ as Saviour and Lord.

The Bluegrass Airport in Lexington, Kentucky, became a scene of witness when two students breezed into the station with an air of radiance and excitement on their countenances. They were returning from a trip to Canada where they had just seen 200 people make commitments for Christ. Recognizing a friend in the crowd, they rushed over to tell him what God had done. Before the boys finished the report, most of the people in the airport lobby had gathered around to listen. Other conversation virtually ceased. The crowd stood enraptured, some with tears in their eyes, to hear told in a new way the old, old story of Jesus and His love.

Typifying this glowing spirit of witness was the college girl going to Cincinnati, Ohio, on a bus. The man seated next to her asked why she was reading her Bible. When she told him about her love for the Word, and spoke about God's plan of redemption, the man was so impressed that he wanted his friend to hear her testimony. So they switched seats, and the girl proceeded to tell her story again. Before she was finished the elderly gentleman in front turned around and asked her to speak louder for he was having difficulty getting every word. By this time the woman across the aisle was interested. So the youth asked if they would like for her to speak so that everyone could hear. Accordingly she stood up behind the driver's seat and gave her witness to all the passengers. When the bus pulled into the Cincinnati terminal, before opening the door, the driver turned to the girl and asked, "Do you have anything more to say?" To which the Asbury student responded, "All I want to say is Hallelujah!"

When face-to-face witness has not been possible other means of communication have been found. In the first hours of the revival, many students used the telephone to call home and plead with parents and pastors to give God a chance in their homes and churches. Students had all the lines out of Wilmore tied up for days. Not every plea met with understanding or found favorable response, but in place after place where these calls were received, revival did come.

One man and his college-age son drove hundreds of miles to tell on the campus how Christ had come into their lives after their daughter and sister had called and witnessed to them.

Two students were especially burdened to share their testimony with one of the most outspoken atheists in the nation. They tried for several minutes to convince her of their sincerity and love, but she only ridiculed them for "robbing me of my constitutional rights" by calling her. She did say that she would be glad to come to the revival if the college would pay her normal speaker's fee of $3,000.

During the late Spring a WATS (Wide Area Toll Service) telephone was installed at the seminary to facilitate continuous communication of the revival across the nation. In service twenty-four hours a day, this long distance line was used to contact individuals, prayer groups and churches in forty-seven states. Often witnesses gathered around the WATS phone and conducted a service just as they would in a church. There was singing, testifying, reading from the Scripture, and prayer. Occasionally one might hear the sound of rejoicing on the other end of the line.

After one such service conducted for a prayer group of a large church in Cincinnati, two ladies came to Asbury to see for themselves what the revival was like. Talking with various people on the campus confirmed their suspicions, and before they ventured home one knelt at the altar to make a full dedication of her life to God.

Almost any person on the Asbury campus could tell of calls received from other persons requesting more information about the revival. Typical was the pastor in Decatur, Illinois, who phoned a seminary professor. As the teacher gave him more complete details of God's working, the pastor became so quiet the professor thought he had been disconnected. Asked if he was still on the line, the pastor sobbed that he was listening but was so overcome that he could not speak.

Out of this telephone report, as in so many others, came a request that a team of students be sent to the church to bear their witness. A carload went shortly afterward, and a revival broke out that lasted for weeks.

Some persons in San Antonio, Texas, called one night to request that prayers be mobilized for the operator of one of the best-known strip-tease clubs in the city. The group which was praying for this man included the owners of San Antonio's largest burlesque night club, closed following their conversion a few weeks before. By means of the WATS phone, in a matter of minutes, a number of people across the nation were called to prayer for this man's salvation.

A few hours later another call came from the Alamo city to report that the man had accepted the Lord and had gone down to "close his strip-tease joint forever."

A call of a different nature—rather humorous when first heard —came from the editor of one of the nation's largest religious periodicals. He had engaged a reporter from a Louisville newspaper to do a story for the magazine. When the report was filed on the revival, the reporter said that he could find no dissident voice on campus, though he had tried. The editor was astounded in view of the magnitude of the movement. So he called a seminary professor to check it out. To his relief, the editor was told that there were indeed a few skeptics around, but that for the moment critics had gone underground. During those first days of the revival it was simply embarrassing for one claiming any degree of objectivity to gainsay the reality of what God was doing.

The short-wave radio has also been an instrument useful to the revival witness. Ham operators used the college transmitter to relay the news to friends around the world. Students whose parents serve abroad in missionary service found it especially convenient. In some instances those contacted in far places have reported back that revival has broken out after they have repeated the story.

Recorded testimonies of the revival have likewise become a means of getting out the message. After one church in Illinois heard a tape of the revival testimonies, twenty-five people came forward to the altar and made a new commitment of their lives to God.

A ham radio operator in Kansas City, Missouri, played a revival tape to another operator in Brazil. He recorded it, played it to his congregation, and to their amazement revival came to this Brazilian congregation.

A similar story is told of a tape played at a meeting in Tegucigalpa, Honduras. Upon hearing the sounds of revival, the group found themselves on their knees seeking the same refreshing wind of the Spirit.

Personal letters have been used to accomplish the same results. One family in Ohio received a letter from a daughter who reported what had happened when God took over the campus. That evening in church they read the letter to the congregation. The Holy Spirit moved mightily upon the people, and a revival began which lasted for days with hundreds of spiritual victories won.

A letter came from an Air Force chaplain in Thailand in which he wrote, "When I read in a letter how God is sending revival at Asbury, my heart was touched, my spirit revived, my faith renewed, and I wept openly as I read it again and again. This Sunday I am going to depart from military routine, lay aside the formal service, and read this letter about the revival. Pray with me that revival will come to my men."

One of hundreds of personal letters to public leaders was sent by an Asbury student to the editor of her home town newspaper. It was printed in the *Citizen Patriot* in Jackson, Michigan.

There is a new kind of demonstration at Asbury during these days of national college sit-ins—not in the administration offices, but in the college and seminary chapels. Students are throwing around a lot of three-, four-, and five-letter words, too. Words like "joy," "love," "pray," and "faith."

The letter went on to tell something about the spontaneous revival, and how students were seeking meaning for their lives and "finding it through faith in Jesus Christ."

They plan to turn the world upside-down, not because they're troublemakers, but for the sake of Jesus Christ! They want to go to other campuses—not to cause a riot but to share the spirit of revival! The demonstration is a demonstration of faith. It is not getting out-of-hand for it is God's hand.

This published letter brings out another means of outreach—the press. Though not a part of the revival community, their reporting of what they saw and felt doubtless has been a notable factor in the transmission of the revival story.

Wanting to do nothing to "sensationalize" the revival, the College Public Relations Office waited a full twenty-four hours from the onset of the movement before making an initial news release. After taking those measures which were normal for any item of news, the college administration organized itself to meet what became an onslaught of reporters from newspapers, magazines, radio, television and the wire services. Daily—and later weekly—

news releases on the latest happenings were prepared for dissemination; and dozens of pictures were made available to the press. Representatives of the Associated Press were on campus daily to observe the proceedings and to interview students, faculty and visitors.

On the second day, television cameramen made their first of many forays into Hughes Auditorium to record video tapes of the tremendous service while in progress. Again, college officials, though allowing the newsmen to move freely, did nothing to stage any special scenes.

One newsman, after getting a story, said that it was heart-warming to report something good for a change. "I'm sick and tired of covering campus riots," he said. Then, as if having an after-thought, he added, "If those kids run out of something to pray for about 2 o'clock in the morning, ask them to pray for me."

Strangely this reverent attitude generally characterized the reporting of the revival. It would have been easy to write articles in a way to suggest ridicule, but such was never done. The appreciative—and at times almost jubilant—reaction of the press appeared to be itself another manifestation of divine control in the movement.

Leading newspapers across America carried the reports. Often the latest news was printed in banner headlines on the front page with three- and four-column pictures. Foreign papers as far away as Singapore picked up news stories from correspondents.

Countless feature articles and editorials were written by men and women who wanted to "tell it like it is" and beyond that to challenge and encourage their readers to stop, read, think and give God a chance.

Perhaps none has said it more succinctly and unforgettably than Don Daniels in his column in the *Wheeling News Register* of February 8, 1970 as follows:

Did you hear about the love-in at Asbury College?

Shucks, I'll bet you never even heard of Asbury College. Or of Wilmore, Kentucky, where it is. And Asbury College is only a short clip shot away from a theological seminary; so it is a kinda unlikely place for a love-in, wouldn't you think.

Let me tell you about it because this is Sunday and as far as I know the love-in is still going on.

It seems that Tuesday morning about 10 o'clock people gathered for a "Testimony Service" at the college chapel. By late Wednesday, much longer than 24 hours later, the service was still going on. This was a love-in for Christ!

Isn't that amazing? And encouraging?

There are about 1,000 students at Asbury College. By Wednesday morning nearly all of them had come to speak their faith. The estimate was that possibly 2,000 persons, many of them townspeople and many from a great distance, had heard the word and joined the throng.

That makes me feel kinda good inside.

And little Asbury College will probably get a paragraph or two from the wire services. After all, nothing happened there. Nobody kidnapped the college president. There wasn't a single window broken in the administration building. The only cops on the scene indulged in prayer and not "brutality."

No news in that, is there?

Except for me. I think there is a lot of news in that. Good, gutty news that tells me there remains on the nation's campuses a hard core sense of morality, and that in the final analysis the mark on history will be written by the people who spurn the podium of militant dissent in favor of a quiet place to talk with God.

Now citizen, it matters little to me what your faith is.

I don't know if Asbury is a Baptist school. The girl who called said only it is a "Christian" school. That's good enough for me. And if a man wants to stand and "testify" and say that he has found a comfort and a strength in his faith then I would have to count myself a fool to laugh or sneer at him.

And I think if a man flings his glove of faith in the face of the howling mob then it must give each of us an inspiration.

I care not if you are Christian or Jew, Hindustani or Buddhist, I must believe that it starts the adrenalin running just a little swifter when a group of young people spontaneously gather in consort to sing whatever Battle Hymn is theirs.

I think it's news. News of the first order.

It is news that in a small Kentucky town maybe a dozen or so miles from Lexington at an obscure little school some young people have offered a vital transfusion for the weary veins of a sometimes staggering nation. It is precisely the type of blood we need.

Someday, I suppose all of the people of the world will come to believe that there is but one God, as most probably they do already. When the time comes that we can all agree on a single name for the Supreme Being we will have at last established that vital key for communication . . . and I presume we will then find a fashion for living under a single banner.

You all know me, a busted down Catholic, a sometimes dissident Christian who drinks too much and smokes too much and favors mini-skirts on everyone but my wife and my sister. So I guess I got no right to even take a distant part of the action from Asbury College.

But it somehow reassures me, I know this, patriot. While

the lion roams the streets and the fires of fury burn in the land, and the wind of conflict sears our cities, I can join no other battle line than that formed by the young people at Asbury College.

I'm gonna get on the side where God is.

"If my people, which are called by my name, humble themselves, and pray, and seek my face, and turn from their wicked ways, then I will hear from heaven, and will forgive their sin, and heal their land" (II Chronicles 7:14 RSV).

7
Crisis and Opportunity

HAROLD SPANN

Now, months after that historic morning of February 3, people are wondering about the future.

Harley Bierce, writing about the Asbury revival in a front-page story in *The Indianapolis Star* wistfully asked, "Could it really be in the last third of the sophisticated, electronic, space-hopping 20th Century, that a great 'spiritual awakening' has begun to sweep America?" The reporter could scarcely believe that "such a thing—without charismatic leadership, without widespread publicity, without emotional gimmicks," could spread "like a prairie fire from mid-America to both oceans."

Yet it is clear that something ignited at Asbury College which is still burning. Without any planned strategy, the revival has seared into the hearts of multiplied thousands of people from coast to coast. It has penetrated to Canada in the North and as far South as Brazil. Its effects have been felt as far away as Japan and Africa.

The way that the movement has spread so quickly underscores a deep hunger for God. There is a worldwide spiritual vacuum today which all our ecclesiastical structures and material affluence have not filled. Multitudes are disillusioned with the superficiality of so much that goes on in the name of religion. Pious platitudes, beautiful ceremonies, and social activism have not satisfied their soul.

While many people have rejected the organized church with its creeds and rules, they will respond to a person who is walking evidence of the transforming power of Jesus Christ. When a thousand young people on a college campus stand and sing "He touched me, O He touched me, and now I am no longer the same," they sing it as a testimony to what has really happened to them and people begin to listen—closely! And when they go out over the land intoxicated with joy to tell with simplicity and faithfulness what great things God has done for them, people begin to seek for the same touch of God upon their own lives.

Here—at the point of spiritual reality—contact can be made with vast numbers of people who are tired of playing church. They may not be religious experts, but they have enough sense to know that God is alive, and they want to know Him in genuine experience. However it may be defined, these honest hearts want revival—the reality of Christ in the inner man that pervades the whole fiber of life.

The Asbury outpouring has brought this experience into dramatic focus. Herein lies the appeal and validity of the movement —not the surprising way it began, nor the unusual pattern of the marathon services. These phenomena, though fascinating, are incidental to the deep, lasting work of the Holy Spirit in the lives of people.

This is what revival is all about: people coming alive to God. Persons frustrated in their own self-centeredness are set free. The heart is made clean. Prayer breathes the air of heaven. The Bible speaks with meaning and authority. Newborn faith lays hold upon the promises of God. Joy fills the heart with singing. Praise of the

Most High pulsates through life. There are still temptations to overcome and sufferings to endure, but through it all, the light of Christ shines through. Jesus is real!

When viewed from the perspective of vital Christianity, actually there is nothing unusual about this experience. The emotional intensity of the moment will fluctuate, but if men lived in the fulness of the Spirit of Christ, as God desires, revival would be a constant reality.

For many people this is the case. Hence it can be said that a deep revival current is always flowing in the spiritual life of the true church. But there are seasons—in the providence of God—when this stream seems to break forth in mighty power, touching great numbers of people. It is during these great movements of revival that the work of the Holy Spirit is brought into boldest relief.

When people remove the roadblocks between them and God, it is not long before barriers with their fellow man are also removed. Revival makes people love each other—not some vague, fickle affection for humanity in general, but rather the definite, abiding love for people as persons.

Exemplifying this spirit was the girl who stood one day in the Asbury auditorium to say in a whisper, "I love you . . . I have laryngitis; I can't speak; I just want to stand here and love you." So she just stood there and smiled at the vast audience for two whole minutes. The message came through.

In such a spirit of love, whether it is on a college or university campus, in a church or community, in government or the nation, reconciliation follows. Grudges are gone, prejudices forgotten. Many a person arose from the altar with a new attitude toward racial problems. Black and white stood side by side and shared their Saviour's love. Divisions were healed between faculty and students. Even the generation gap seemed to evaporate. One eighty-year-old grandmother expressed the secret pretty well when she testified like a teen-ager, "I'm high on Jesus."

Where this feeling abounds minor differences between church bodies also become unimportant. It would have seemed ridiculous to have asked a fellow worshiper in those days of revival if he were a Baptist or a Methodist, Calvinist or Arminian, Protestant or Catholic. In the fellowship of the Spirit, Jesus Christ is Lord of all!

Those of us concerned about ecumenical relations should take note of this. The Asbury revival has made it clear that Christian unity comes in Pentecost. If we seek it in any other way, as through superorganization or merger, we are only fooling ourselves.

Out of revival comes the dynamic for a compelling evangelism and social concern. Christians are gripped by a consciousness of the "love that will not let them go." Constrained by this experience, they reach out to get hold of their fellow men with a love that will not let them go. No person is too low, no place too insignificant for them to go.

Since the revival's beginning, thousands of people have become involved in various kinds of redemptive ministry. Some visit homes for the aged; some work with delinquents and school dropouts; some are becoming more active in community affairs. One day scores of seminary students went out to clean up a garbage dump, sweep the streets, and paint a widow's house.

Most impressive has been the way people have fanned out across the nation to share their testimony. Some weekends as many as two-thirds of the Asbury student body were away on these witness excursions. Where they have gone, others have caught the vision. By now a veritable army of people have seen God use them in this way.

To a remarkable degree, the revival has given practical substance to the New Testament concept of the priesthood of all believers. Distinctions between clergy and laity have all but vanished. People are learning as never before that they can and must minister as servants of Christ.

Usually they are not gifted speakers; nor are they especially well trained in methods of evangelism. Yet people marvel at their ability to communicate. The sincerity and earnestness of their approach command respect. They know whereof they speak, and they are not afraid to say it. As one witness boldly affirmed, "I feel like Paul walking into a city with the message of God."

Even more refreshing, youth are primarily doing the talking—that group sometimes wrongly dismissed as "the lost generation." More than their parents, they are willing to throw caution to the wind and get out with the gospel "where the action is." God is showing us the powerful potential of young people whose boundless energies and contagious enthusiasm have been released for good through a moment of divine encounter with Him.

Let no one think that every problem has been solved or is being solved by this present spiritual awakening. Not every person is revived. Not every human circumstance is penetrated. Some refuse to heed the call of God. Some choose their own way rather than His.

Revival does not mean that man's humanity is overthrown nor his will pre-empted by God. But revival gives to man a new perception of his weakness. Man sees that, after all, he is but a creature of flesh, finally dependent upon God alone. In recognition of his helplessness, man knows the futility of living to and for himself. Those things that matter in eternity begin to come into view. Human plans and schedules and calendars fade into the background. Christ becomes the Lord of life, and before Him every knee must bow.

Overshadowing it all is the commanding sense of the Divine

Presence. A revived seminarian summed it up in one word, *Immanuel*—"God with us." So great was this feeling that when three cultured ladies from Chattanooga walked into the back of Hughes Auditorium, one of them said, "I must take off my shoes, for this is holy ground." She did and her two companions did likewise. In their stocking feet they walked forward and knelt at the altar for prayer.

It is not impertinent to ask, "But *why* at Asbury?" After all it is a small college in a somewhat obscure village tucked away in a rather remote section of the country. If one drew any conclusion about revival from Asbury's location, it would have to be in its unpretentious circumstance. One Texas pastor said, after visiting the campus for the first time, "Why it is so insignificant that it *is* significant."

In point of fact, of course, what happened at Asbury in other ways has occurred in many places. But this observation only enhances the question why movements of the Spirit on this scale seem to come in some places and some periods more than others. Probably there is no adequate answer. We must acknowledge that it is a mystery. What God does in revival, finally, is by His own sovereign choice. No man can explain it; still less can he ever take any credit for what is done. In the presence of revival, one does not need to understand—only to take off his shoes.

Nevertheless, the mighty power by which God breaks through human impotence is not inconsistent with His Word. Though revivals are a display of supernatural grace, they are given by God when His will is sought by man.

Underlying this condition is the recognition of divine authority. There is little point in talking about revival unless we believe what God says. If there is some doubt about the integrity of His Word, there is likely to be little concern for people to measure their lives by it. For this reason theological positions which discredit the Holy Scriptures never produce revival.

It is, therefore, very significant that the present movement of revival has emerged in evangelical colleges. This does not imply that these schools have measured up to all their professions. But at least they revere the Bible and acknowledge its precepts as the rule of life. Such faith provides a setting conducive to spiritual sensitiveness and perception. Where the movement has spread to some secular campuses and liberal churches, invariably it has come through groups of witnesses imbued with an evangelical spirit.

The Word written in the Bible reveals the living Word in our midst—Jesus Christ. As He is lifted up, we see how far short our own lives have fallen. The props of self-sufficiency are knocked down. We are found out for what we are—sinners.

Repentance is a complete house cleaning. There can be no compromise with sin. God will not put the beauty of His holiness on the bargain counter of man's carnal market place at a reduced price! Anything known to be an impediment to our character in Christ must be removed. The thousands of confessions these last months have been characterized by a fear of pretense. Again and again people have bared their souls. It has not been easy. Most of us have had to make confessions, but we have learned anew that God's love shines only through broken and contrite spirits.

It has been seen, too, how self-disclosure in one person encourages another troubled heart to be honest. Also by sharing our weaknesses we are drawn closer to each other for strength.

When one's heart is free, then the Spirit of Jesus can flow through in holy intercession. Such praying becomes more intense as the burden increases. It will bring one to the cross. It will make him search his motives. It will lead one to make himself available for God to use as He pleases.

In such prayer one most completely enters into the mystery of what God does in revival. Jesus has said: "Whatsoever you ask in My Name, I will do it . . ." (John 14:13 RSV). How God answers one's supplications lies in the jurisdiction of His own perfect will, but assurance is given that in His will, nothing is impossible.

Much prayer had been offered for revival at Asbury. For years some had been fervently interceding. A time of turmoil on the campus two years before accentuated this concern. In addition to the thousands of God's people holding up the schools in their private devotions, there were numbers of prayer groups in the community church, and on both college and seminary campuses. A series of revival services at the local United Methodist Church in January deepened the burden.

As events have unfolded since February 3, it has become apparent that the extent of prayer for revival was far greater than anyone then knew. Again and again persons have told of unusual promptings to pray for Asbury, some in most unexpected places. For example, a pastor of a small Quaker Church in Ohio related how early this year this impulse suddenly came upon him. It was strange because neither he nor his family have any direct relation to Asbury. Yet so persistent was the impression that he mentioned it to his wife, and the two took the burden to the Lord. A few days later he read in the newspaper of the mighty revival at Asbury. Checking back he found that it began soon after he felt the burden to pray.

If the full story were ever to be known, doubtless there were hundreds, if not thousands, of burdened people like this around the world on their knees pleading for Asbury. The same could be said of every other place that has known great revival. They will never be known on this earth, but their prayers have been heard in heaven.

That is the way revival comes. It starts as people pray. Their numbers may not be large in the beginning. In schools and churches across the land, it has been shown that revival begins with the few who care. But as they get the channels open to the throne of God, and share His love with others, revival spreads from the center to the circumference in an ever-widening circle of flaming witness.

A glimpse of what this means has been given through the events reported in this book. Undoubtedly what has been told is only a small part of God's movement through many avenues of revival in our day. The external mode and expression may vary from place to place and from person to person. But the deep, abiding reality of the Divine Presence is the same.

The hope is that this experience, however manifest, will envelop the church. There does not appear to be any other solution to the complexity of problems that surround us.

Our day is one of confusion and disillusionment. The optimism of the early part of the twentieth century has been destroyed by the harsh realities of a warring world. The question in the theological circles now is whether there is any basis for hope. The theologians search. The secular world wonders. The institutions which have been the heart of our society and our glory are now under brutal attack. The foundations tremble. Old norms are challenged. Many want to determine their own laws. The darkness has deepened and man has lost his way. Worse—he has lost his nerve.

Man has tried his best devices. They have failed. Perhaps the despair of finding any human way of deliverance, coupled with the threat of impending catastrophe, will bring men to *face* reality. It has happened before. In fact, the greatest national revivals of the past have come during the darkest periods of church history. In such hours of hopelessness, men have looked up in the night and found the stars still shining. Sometimes these awakenings have saved the nation from disaster. In other times they have prepared the church to face judgments to come.

What it will be in our generation, no one now can say, but the Almighty has come to stand in the midst of the clamor and turmoil of the world to repeat His invitation.

If my people which are called by my name, humble themselves and pray, and seek my face, and turn from their wicked ways, then I will hear from heaven, and will forgive their sin, and heal their land (2 Chronicles 7:14 RSV).

Now is the hour of decision. Man must bring himself to participate in a divine moment of redeeming grace. No one can afford to gamble on when this opportunity may end, or what the future holds. Finally the future holds nothing but God.

Appendix

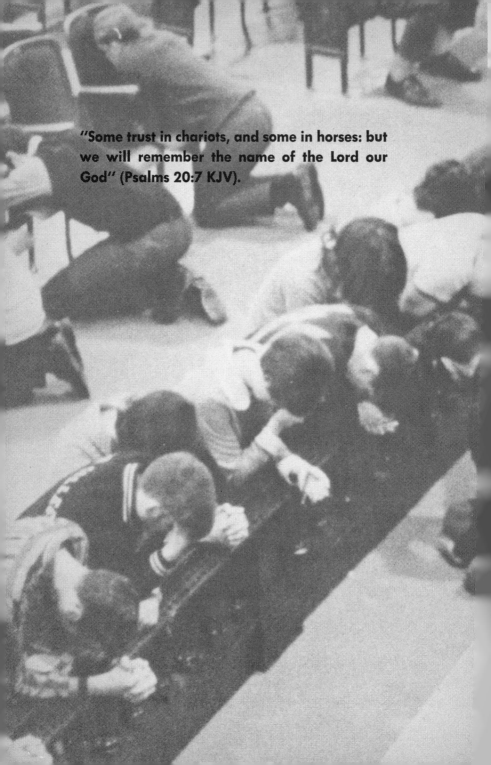

"Some trust in chariots, and some in horses: but we will remember the name of the Lord our God" (Psalms 20:7 KJV).

Appendix
Campus Roots for Revival

DENNIS F. KINLAW

The most beneficent influences in our society have found their inception in a moment when God acts. To a revived heart, truth becomes more than an idea. It is a vital reality which must be translated into life. That is why the moral earnestness of revival converts had much to do with the abolition of slavery, the temperance movement, a growing concern for child welfare, medical aid for the sick, education for all, women's suffrage, the reclamation of the socially lost such as the prostitute and the criminal, and the giving of the gospel to those where its truth had never gone. When God comes in a moment of quickening illumination, the results are large and the shadow long.

Unfortunately, modern church leaders have been more enamored of the by-products of revival than by the saving activity that made them possible. It seems that when man's view of eternity is dimmed, he may still be able to see the relevance of the temporal accompaniments.

Our generation needs again to examine the root of our heritage, not just its fruit. From the days of the Puritan fathers, who insisted upon a personal experience of conversion before admission to membership in the church, American life has been permeated by an evangelicalism that not only has valued revival but has demanded it for its own maintenance. This has given to American life much of the "soul" that it has exhibited through the years. Its values, its ideals, its sensitivities have been deeply informed by spiritual revival. Even those who decry "revivalism" admit this influence.

It may come as a surprise to some today, but not to any American historian, that the concern for higher education on this continent was rooted in spiritual revival. When the Spirit of God touches a man's heart and renews it, there is an accompanying effect upon the mind. The quickening of the Spirit affects the intellect as well as the soul. The result is a hunger for knowledge, for truth, and for an understanding of the relationship between the two. This impulse finds added strength in the revival emphasis upon the Christian's responsibility as a priest of God, and the corresponding need to be trained in the Scriptures in order to fulfill this ministry.

It is no accident then that American revivalism has been closely related to the American campuses. William Warren Sweet points out in *Revivalism in America* that six of the nine colonial colleges of the United States established before 1769 had some relationship directly or indirectly to the great revivals that swept the American colonies.

Princeton University is a case in point. Founded in 1746 as a child of Presbyterian revivalism, its chief purpose was to prepare young men to carry on the revival witness. Its first five presidents were all outstanding revival preachers. For years this school sent out men burning with a zeal for evangelism. Their witness flavored large segments of the Presbyterian Church.

To mention the names of colleges and universities that were either the by-products of revival or heavily influenced by revival is to list most of the great names in the early history of higher education: Yale (Conn.), Brown (R.I.), Dartmouth (N.H.), Rutgers (N.J.), Columbia (N.Y.), Hampden-Sydney (Va.), Williams (Mass.), the University of Pennsylvania, Washington and Lee (Va.), Allegheny (Penna.), Oberlin (Ohio), Bucknell (Pa.), to mention a few.

It was largely the revivalistic denominations that sprinkled the landscape of nineteenth century America with academic institutions. The Methodist and Baptists are the chief examples. Both are strongly revivalistic and between them they established fifty-five colleges across the nation between 1830 and 1861. Sweet states that during the first half of the nineteenth century an overwhelming majority of the colleges founded west of the Allegheny Mountains "were established and fostered by the revivalistic Churches, and in all of them revivalism was kept continuously alive." Many of these schools are now among the most highly respected of our institutions of higher learning.

In keeping with this heritage, revivals have been familiar experiences in American colleges. In 1802, for example, a great awakening came to Yale. Under the preaching of its president, one-third of the students were converted, and thirty became ordained ministers of the Gospel. The whole life of the college was changed. What happened there was characteristic of similar revivals at the same time at Amherst (Mass.), Dartmouth and Williams.

The revivals at Asbury and many other colleges today belong to this tradition. In a profound sense, they call attention to those basic priorities which give direction and purpose to all intellectual pursuit. The revivals also show clearly that academic pursuits need not detract from vital piety.

One of the marks of a visitation of God is that those who participate sense the authenticity and the truth of the movement. But for those who are not involved, who only hear from the lips of another, the report may seem dismissable. Those in the midst of revival find it is self-authenticating. No man need be introduced to his Maker when He comes. Perhaps this may be one of the reasons why revival usually makes large inroads into the youth of a community. Their desire for reality finds here its satisfaction. The result is that again and again the leaders in revival have been the young.

Today there is much discussion of student power. Many talk as if this were something new. A realistic look at the history of Christianity will teach that it has always attracted the young and that they have always wielded great power. Jesus Himself was only in His early thirties when He died. His major disciples were young people by today's standards. Throughout the history of the church, youth have rallied to His challenge. Not only have they found something authentic to meet their inner needs, but they have found a sense of mission that has given eternal purpose and meaning to life. In a moment of confrontation with Christ, they have found their reason for living.

Illustrative of this is the story of the beginning of the modern American missionary movement. Perhaps the most significant single event in that incredible story is the meeting of two sophomores and three freshmen from Williams College in what was later to be known as "the Haystack Prayer Meeting."

Or consider the meeting in the summer of 1886 when 251 collegians gathered from various colleges and universities of America to spend four weeks in prayer and Bible study with D. L. Moody. When the group gathered, there were three young men who already had become concerned about the evangelism of the world. During the next four weeks the moment of call came to ninety-seven others. From this group came the Student Volunteer Movement, with its passion for winning the world for Christ, which ultimately led to the planting of missionaries from its membership around the world. The names of John R. Mott, Robert Speer, Robert Wilder, Samuel Zwemer bring to the minds of those who know the story the memory of the stream of influence that emanated from those students. So great was that impact that it helped to change the character of world history in the twentieth century. The full story of the influence of these young men and their followers on the social, political, educational and charitable institutions of the world—to say nothing of the religious—has yet to be written.

The twentieth century has been one in which the map of the earth has been transformed. To some extent this has been due to military conquest; however, most of the change has been due to the conquest of ideas. Concepts of equality, brotherhood, human dignity and freedom have created aspirations in the minds and breasts of the peoples of the earth.

These ideas were not indigenous to all the nations of mankind. Most of them were carried first across the world by the members of the Haystack Prayer Meeting and the young men who met with Moody and the successors of both groups. The world took little notice of either of those student meetings, yet the final history of the twentieth century may refer to both of these as decisive moments. When God comes to visit His people, that moment is never an end. God comes and something begins. The shadows that are cast are not just longer. They may be eternal.

That is why many are thanking God for the revivals that have come to so many schools and churches during these last months. More than anyone can now estimate, these acts of God are among the most meaningful events of our time.

Revival in Our Nation: An Interpretation

L. JACK GRAY

REVIVAL IS HERE! To make such affirmation at this stage may seem about as questionable or as convincing as it would have been to have announced, "Judgment has come!" on the day Noah laid the keel of the ark; or "The Reformation is on," on the day Luther nailed his ninety-five Theses to the door; or to declare, "The World Mission Movement is launched," when William Carey preached his famous missionary sermon from Isaiah 54:2,3, saying, "Expect great things from God, attempt great things for God." But, nevertheless, *"REVIVAL IS HERE!"*

This is just the beginning! While God has permitted us to walk with Him in new heights, we believe that we are just in the foothills. The exalted peaks of the mountain range of greater things lie ahead.

February 3-10, 1970, Asbury College and Asbury Theological Seminary, Wilmore, Kentucky, will probably be the date and name historians attach to the beginning of this period of revival. Kindred works of God have taken place in many other churches and communities, and within smaller groups on colleges, university and seminary campuses. Because the movement is still new, spontaneous, and not confined to any given denomination or geographical area, national secular news media and denominationally oriented periodicals are presently saying relatively little about a revival movement, but we believe this will come. There are several characteristics of this revival:

This is a revival of *divine initiative*. The events at Asbury, February 3-10, 1970, were so unique, unplanned, powerful—and even unexpected—that both veteran Christian leaders and professional secular reporters saw it as the work of God—a special visitation from heaven.

Revival at Southwestern Baptist Seminary was both unscheduled and unreported. There was only one twenty-minute exposure to a large assembly of seminarians, and that took place in Truett Auditorium on brief notice following chapel at the coffee-break time. The Spirit of God did His work in small groups (about 200) on a Monday evening in the Preaching Chapel, in classes, in spontaneous prayer groups, many dorm rooms and personal conferences. Scheduled, programmed and formal calendar events established particularly for the purpose of revival seemed to be by-passed by the Lord. All who were privileged to be involved in the events of March, 1970, were convinced both by what God did and how He did it, that we had experienced a unique "interruption" initiated by God Himself.

Divine initiative is the Biblical pattern. God initiated audience with Adam who was hiding; Adam was not seeking God. God initiated the Flood in Noah's generation; the preaching of Noah and building of the Ark were but man's preparation for what God assured them He was sending. Pentecost had been scheduled from eternity and announced as far back as Joel; prayer and ten days of tarrying by the upper room crowd prepared them to receive what God had initiated.

Many leaders, established churches, institutions and organizations are responding to God's initiative in revival and becoming His agents of spreading it. But the revival of today, so far as we can discern, was on no denomination's or institution's calendar. This is a revival of *divine initiative*.

This is a revival of the *sovereignty of God*. God profoundly demonstrated His sovereign presence in the Asbury Revival. This He has continued to do through the ministry of hundreds from both the college and seminary. Armed with the simple affirmation, "Jesus is Lord," a brief report of what God did at Wilmore, and a personal testimony, Asbury witnesses have been fanning out across the U.S. In many services the traditional order and content of worship (songs, Scripture reading, sermon, formal invitation) is changed. Even when revival breaks out on campuses or in churches, Christian leaders usually occupy minimal roles. The significance of human instruments is being put in healthy perspective.

In these revival services, the time given to platform witness and invitation is adjusted. The usual fifty-five minute program directed from the pulpit by a pastor and musician and followed by a five minute invitation sometimes becomes a ten or fifteen minute report and personal testimony from the pulpit followed by a one- or two-hour decision time which develops under witness from the people and the power of the Holy Spirit.

In the Southwestern Baptist Seminary revival (which seems to be representative), the variety of decisions made, numbers of people involved and the spontaneous way they responded without anyone having preached or given specific instructions, clearly magnified that the Sovereign Lord was demanding and receiving private audience with individuals. The intensely personal and encouragingly discreet statements which people stood and made, the profound encounters with God which they described, and the pos-

115

itive possession of great release, radiant joy and victory drove home the assurance that God was doing an historic and unique work in His own way on His own terms.

This is a revival of *cleansing the churches.* It is God's sovereign initiative among His people. Cleansing of the churches is evidenced in several ways in particular: one, revival of some members; two, redemption of other members; three, encouragement of the most faithful; and four, judgment of all who make no response.

Revival is being experienced by some church folk who may have been members for years and rather faithful attenders and supporters. New depth of conviction of sin and repentance within the church is common. We are all familiar with conviction of sin born primarily of a pricked conscience, or that motivated by one having found himself below the norm of a local church, or that drawn out by an especially direct sermon, or even that touched by the sharp edge of a portion of Scripture. But we are seeing today a depth of conviction, a candor in confession, and a thoroughness of repentance that surpasses the norms of the past two or three decades. This is the kind that reflects marked kinship to the experience of Peter when "the Lord turned and looked at" him in the hour of his denial, and he "went out, and wept bitterly" (Luke 22:61-62 RSV). Those involved experience spiritual purging. As one woman described herself, "I never felt so clean in my life."

Church members, some of them respected and dependable officers, are being converted: a pastor's wife, a deacon who was also treasurer and Sunday school superintendent, a pastor's college daughter, theological students, other church staff members. (These are all specific persons.)

An element of surprise accompanies these experiences because in the various services in which such decisions were made, no leader called for such a broad spectrum of responses. The quiet, intuitive probing of the Spirit of God had wrought His cleansing work.

This is a revival of the *people's witness*. The personal testimonies shared from the assembly floor in the moments of experience and under evident tutelage of the Holy Spirit is one of the hallmarks of this revival. As reported, the verbal beginnings of the Asbury revival came from the pew in a moving personal testimony. Even witness shared from the pulpit is often the telling of the speaker's experience in the pew. And, uniquely, when pulpit witness is borne and opportunity is opened for public response, the chief witnessing service comes not from the preacher, but the people. The Holy Spirit uses the testimony of each succeeding participant as a probing word of counsel to many others. It becomes a people's service moving informally, powerfully and clearly under the superintendency of the Spirit of God.

This is a revival of *loving fellowship*. Church and student groups who move through such a season of profound renewal, having been humbled before God and humiliated before each other, enter the bonds of warm love and a cohesive fellowship. There is a healthy wholeness about this fellowship. It centers primarily in the Person of Christ Jesus who, all know, has done a great work in them and among them. It is kept balanced in emotion and intellect and theory and practice by being grounded in the Bible and by stronger place being given the Holy Spirit. The opaqueness revealed in unreserved confessions and shattering repentance assures the participants of acceptance by the group. Masks are gone, the real self is out, integrity is restored. But it is not just a quiet, unverbalized fellowship—a witness of joyous sharing is begun which becomes a way of life. The revived ones seek each other out, both privately and publicly, in order to tell what God is continuing to do. This current, living, vitality is an integral part of today's revival.

This is a revival of *young people*. While many adults are involved, the numerical strength of both renewed Christians and redeemed lost people is made up of largely junior high, high-school and college youth.

The current social, moral, political and spiritual upheaval in our nation in particular and in the world in general has produced an unanchored generation of youth. These conditions have put American young people "up for grabs." They are ripe for commitment to something. God is powerfully blessing Christian witness addressed to youth groups in churches, junior high and high schools, and college and university campuses.

A final word about the meaning of revival in our nation. Three possible reasons have been offered for God's historic intervention into the American scene with another spiritual awakening. The first one has been offered by some retired missionaries who participated in the great revivals in China in the 1930s. Against the backdrop of that national experience they suggest that God may be purging churches in the United States to prepare us for a national tragedy, even a world communist takeover. God forbid!

A second, and much happier, interpretation is that He is getting us ready for the return of the Lord. Until revival takes on international proportions, we find it difficult to relate it to the Second Coming of our Lord. But, revival may encompass the world, so, let us hope, pray and work!

A third reason given for a heavenly visitation on the American church scene is that the Spirit of God is getting us ready for the evangelization of the nation such as began on our eastern seaboard in 1858, and was followed by the greatest movement of evangelizing a nation and world mission outreach in the history of Christendom. How urgently this is needed! Our hearts leap with joy at the prospect.

But *REVIVAL IS HERE!* And when God grants revival to some, He makes all responsible to receive it.

Bibliography

Bibliography

Wire Service Releases for All News Media
Many newspapers in America carried portions or all of the releases of the Associated Press on February 5, 6, 7, 9, 10, 23, March 4, and May 14, 1970. United Press International issued a release on April 23, 1970; and The Evangelical Press Association, February 14, 1970.

Selected Feature Stories in Major Newspapers

In addition to the regular news coverage of the wire services, some papers covered the revival in feature articles, usually written by a staff correspondent. Most stories had some local reference. Some had a larger reference to the religious life across the nation.

Chattanooga (Tennessee) *News,* March 14, 17, 1970.
The Chicago Tribune, April 12, 1970.
The Cleveland Press, May 2, 1970; May 18, 1970.
The Columbus (Ohio) *Citizen-Journal,* July 4, 1970.
Flint (Michigan) *Journal,* March 14, 1970.

Harrisburg (Pennsylvania) *Evening News,* April 28, 1970.

The Indianapolis Star, February 23, 1970.

Kankakee (Illinois) *Daily Journal,* February 10, 1970.

Lexington (Kentucky) *Herald,* February 5, 6, 7, 8, 10, 14, 18, 24, March 19, May 26, 1970.

Lexington (Kentucky) *Leader,* February 4, 5, 6, 7, 8, 9, 11, 13, 14, 18, 23, 27; March 6, 10, 11, 20; May 14, 16, 1970.

Louisville Courier-Journal, February 5, 6, 7, 8, 14, 1970.

Louisville Times, February 5, 6, 7, 16, 24, March 9, 1970.

Michigan State News, East Lansing, Michigan, February 20, 1970.

Middletown (Ohio) *Journal,* March 1, 4, 6, 1970.

Muskegon (Michigan) *Chronicle,* February 28, 1970.

Nashville (Tennessee) *Banner,* May 12, 1970.

Nashville (Tennessee) *Tennessean,* July 14, 1970.

Parkersburg (West Virginia) *Sentinel,* March 14, 1970.

Pittsburgh Press, March 10, 16, 1970.

St. Louis Post-Dispatch, May 24, 1970.

Seattle Times, March 25, April 25, 1970.

Singapore Eastern Sun, March 25, 1970.

Valdosta (Georgia) *Daily Times,* March 11, 1970.

Wheeling (West Virginia) *News-Register,* February 8, 1970.

Wichita (Kansas) *Eagle,* May 5, 1970.

Selected Articles and News Accounts in Periodicals

Airut (Finnish Herald International), June, 1970.

The Alliance Witness, April 29, 1970.

Christian Life, April, 1970.

Christianity Today, February 27, March 13, April 10, 1970.

Decision, May, 1970.

Eternity, June, 1970.

Evangelical Beacon, April 7, 1970.

The Free Methodist, March 10, 31, May 26, 1970.

Good News, April-June, 1970.

The Herald, February 25, March 11, 25, April 8, May 6, 20.

Herald of Holiness, March 25, April 8, June 3, July 8, 1970.

Interpreter, February, 1970.

Light and Life, July 14, 1970.

Light of Life, March, 1970.

The Missionary Standard, April, 1970; June, 1970.

Missionary Tidings, May, 1970.

Moody Monthly, May, June, July-August, 1970.

National Enquirer, June 28, 1970.

Thrust, April, 1970.

United Evangelical Action, Spring, 1970.

The War Cry, March 7, March 14, 1970.

The Wesleyan Advocate, April 6, 20, 1970.

Vital Christianity, April 29, May 3, 1970.

Voice of Evangelical Methodism, March, April, June-July, 1970.

World Vision Magazine, May, 1970

Publications of Asbury College and Asbury Seminary

The Asbury *Collegian,* February 25, April 8, May 13, 1970.

Asbury College *Alumnus,* February, April, 1970.

Short Circuit, March 5, 1970.

Asbury Seminary *Advocate,* March, 1970.

Reference Material

Sweet, William Warren, *Revivalism in America,* New York: Charles Scribner's Sons, 1944.